# GUID ... ES

C000117219

Edited by **Helen Paynter** and **David Spriggs**

**The Bible Reading Fellowship**
15 The Chambers, Vineyard
Abingdon OX14 3FE
**brf.org.uk**

The Bible Reading Fellowship (BRF) is a Registered Charity (233280)

ISBN 978 1 80039 036 2
All rights reserved

This edition © The Bible Reading Fellowship 2021
Cover image © iStock.com/royaltystockphoto

Distributed in Australia by:
MediaCom Education Inc, PO Box 610, Unley, SA 5061
Tel: 1 800 811 311 | admin@mediacom.org.au

Distributed in New Zealand by:
Scripture Union Wholesale, PO Box 760, Wellington
Tel: 04 385 0421 | suwholesale@clear.net.nz

### Acknowledgements

Scripture quotations marked with the following abbreviations are taken from the version shown. Where no abbreviation is given, the quotation is taken from the version stated in the contributor's introduction. NRSV: The New Revised Standard Version of the Bible, Anglicised edition, copyright © 1989, 1995 by the Division of Christian Education of the National Council of the Churches of Christ in the United States of America. Used by permission. All rights reserved. NIV: The Holy Bible, New International Version (Anglicised edition) copyright © 1979, 1984, 2011 by Biblica. Used by permission of Hodder & Stoughton Publishers, a Hachette UK company. All rights reserved. 'NIV' is a registered trademark of Biblica. UK trademark number 1448790. ESV: The Holy Bible, English Standard Version, published by HarperCollins Publishers, © 2001 Crossway Bibles, a division of Good News Publishers. Used by permission. All rights reserved.

Every effort has been made to trace and contact copyright owners for material used in this resource. We apologise for any inadvertent omissions or errors, and would ask those concerned to contact us so that full acknowledgement can be made in the future.

A catalogue record for this book is available from the British Library

Printed by Gutenberg Press, Tarxien, Malta

# Suggestions for using *Guidelines*

Set aside a regular time and place, if possible, when and where you can read and pray undisturbed. Before you begin, take time to be still and, if you find it helpful, use the BRF Prayer on page 6.

In *Guidelines*, the introductory section provides context for the passages or themes to be studied, while the units of comment can be used daily, weekly or whatever best fits your timetable. You will need a Bible (more than one if you want to compare different translations) as Bible passages are not included. Please don't be tempted to skip the Bible reading because you know the passage well. We will have utterly failed if we don't bring our readers into engagement with the word of God. At the end of each week is a 'Guidelines' section, offering further thoughts about or practical application of what you have been studying.

Occasionally, you may read something in *Guidelines* that you find particularly challenging, even uncomfortable. This is inevitable in a series of notes which draws on a wide spectrum of contributors and doesn't believe in ducking difficult issues. Indeed, we believe that *Guidelines* readers much prefer thought-provoking material to a bland diet that only confirms what they already think.

If you do disagree with a contributor, you may find it helpful to go through these three steps. First, think about why you feel uncomfortable. Perhaps this is an idea that is new to you, or you are not happy about the way something has been expressed. Or there may be something more substantial – you may feel that the writer is guilty of sweeping generalisation, factual error, or theological or ethical misjudgement. Second, pray that God would use this disagreement to teach you more about his word and about yourself. Third, have a deeper read about the issue. There are further reading suggestions at the end of each writer's block of notes. And then, do feel free to write to the contributor or the editor of *Guidelines*. We welcome communication, by email, phone or letter, as it enables us to discover what has been useful, challenging or infuriating for our readers. We don't always promise to change things, but we will always listen and think about your ideas, complaints or suggestions. Thank you!

To send feedback, please email **enquiries@brf.org.uk**, phone **+44 (0)1865 319700** or write to the address shown opposite.

# Writers in this issue

**Pauline Hoggarth** was born in Peru. She taught modern languages in Scotland and London before serving with Scripture Union in three different roles in the UK and overseas. She is the author of *The Seed and the Soil* (Langham, 2011).

**Steve Motyer** is a visiting lecturer at London School of Theology, where before his retirement in 2016 he both taught New Testament for many years and ran the Theology and Counselling programme.

**Walter Moberly** is a professor in the Department of Theology and Religion at Durham University. He has recently written *The Bible in a Disenchanted Age* and *The God of the Old Testament* (both Baker Academic).

**Tim Davy** teaches at Redcliffe College, focusing on reading scripture missionally and on vulnerable children. He is involved with Home for Good, and has also helped set up an educational mentoring scheme with Gloucestershire Action for Refugees and Asylum Seekers.

**Richard Martin** served with the Church Army and was the bishop of Rochester's advisor for interfaith concerns. He now is priest-in-charge of three parishes in the Gloucester diocese and is a Third Order Franciscan.

**Bill Goodman** encourages and enables lifelong learning in the Anglican diocese of Sheffield. *Yearning for You*, the published version of his PhD, is a conversation between the Psalms, Song of Songs and contemporary songs. He's also written Advent and Lent courses (available at **lightsforchrist.uk**).

**Stephen Finamore** is principal of Bristol Baptist College. He is married to Rebecca and has two daughters. Steve has worked as a pastor, a lawyer and in community development in inner London and the Peruvian Andes.

**David Spriggs** is a Baptist minister who, following three pastorates, worked for the Evangelical Alliance and Bible Society. He has also written some books and edited *Guidelines* for a few years. During the last nine years, in his 'retirement' he has been minister at two Leicestershire Baptist churches.

**Jenny Hellyer** is a spiritual director, musician, clergy wife and mother based in Eynsham, near Oxford. After teaching and theological study she was part of the Lee Abbey Community in Devon for seven years.

**Hazel Sherman** is a Baptist minister, currently serving in a hybrid role as one of the ministers of West Worthing Baptist Church and a chaplain in the Western Sussex Hospitals NHS Foundation Trust. She has maintained a strong interest in the practice of theology and biblical studies.

# Helen Paynter writes...

In 2012 I spent three weeks in Kolkata, India. Kolkata is the heartland of Kali worship, and during my trip I had the opportunity to visit the Kali temple during the Bengali New Year festivities. I will never forget my experience there. The temple was very busy, and people were clamouring around the idol, with gifts of money, fruit or flowers in their hands. They were praying to the goddess for good luck in the new year. Their desperation and spiritual hunger really saddened me, because they were praying to a god that could never hear and would never reply.

The psalmist (135) may have had a similar experience, since he writes about the idols of the nations that have eyes which cannot see, ears that cannot hear – and mouths that cannot speak. Again and again in scripture the testimony is clear: our God is a speaking God.

The book of Hebrews describes God speaking at many times and in various ways: through the prophets, but ultimately through the Son. The fourth gospel famously begins by describing that Son as the Logos, the Word of God. And it is to this Word that scripture testifies. Because in his mercy, God has not left us with handed-down stories, like some great game of Chinese whispers. He has left us with a written word, through which God still speaks today.

Our contributors are all passionate about the ways in which God speaks today through his word, and once again I am thrilled to offer you this collection of thought-provoking, challenging and inspiring contributions. The Old Testament books we will be studying this season have a focus on the prophets. Bill Goodman takes us through Daniel, Walter Moberly leads us through Isaiah 40—55, and Hazel Sherman offers a week on Malachi. Pauline Hoggarth also takes us through the book of Nehemiah. In the New Testament, Steve Motyer concludes his series in Mark's gospel, and Stephen Finamore takes us through the second half of the book of Revelation. We also have some themed readings, as usual. This includes two weeks for reflection on Advent: David Spriggs invites us to reflect on visitors within the gospel birth accounts, and Jenny Hellyer offers a series of meditations based around the theme of hope. And finally, I'd like to introduce two new contributors. Tim Davy, based at Redcliffe College, offers a week of reflections on vulnerable children in the Old Testament. And Richard Martin, a priest in the Gloucester diocese, gives a thought-provoking series of reflections on interfaith engagement.

Once again I am delighted with the range and depth of contributions that we have on offer. I trust that as you use them, you will be blessed by the speaking God, and prepare well to receive in your hearts once more his incarnate Son, who is his living Word.

# The BRF Prayer

*Almighty God,*
*you have taught us that your word is a lamp for our feet*
*and a light for our path. Help us, and all who prayerfully*
*read your word, to deepen our fellowship with you*
*and with each other through your love.*
*And in so doing may we come to know you more fully,*
*love you more truly, and follow more faithfully*
*in the steps of your son Jesus Christ, who lives and reigns*
*with you and the Holy Spirit, one God forevermore.*
*Amen*

# Nehemiah

## Pauline Hoggarth

'The current coronavirus pandemic represents a unique opportunity for us to rethink our way of inhabiting the Common Home; the way we produce, consume and relate to nature.' These words from Leonardo Boff, Brazilian theologian and activist, writing in March 2020, express an understanding of the pandemic as an opportunity to imagine a different way of living – in commitment to the common good, through neighbourly relationships and rebuilding, both literal and metaphorical (Boff, *Novenanews*, March 2020).

Nehemiah, whose great adventure in leadership we explore over the next two weeks, shares common ground with Boff and others who understand the crisis of the pandemic as, in part at least, a God-given opportunity to live and relate differently on a local and global scale.

In the Hebrew scriptures, Ezra and Nehemiah are one continuous book that tells the story of three missions aimed at restoring the post-exilic Jewish community in Judah following the catastrophe of conquest and exile. After the rebuilding of the Jerusalem temple narrated in Ezra 1—6 and the restoration of the community, in terms of their identity as God's people, in Ezra 7—10, Nehemiah's account details the rebuilding of the city walls, the repopulation of the city and how the community, with the encouragement of both Ezra and Nehemiah, renewed their commitment to covenant relationship with God.

The current pandemic has also shone a spotlight on the kind of leadership that is effective in crisis situations. Nehemiah has often been appropriated by the church as a model of leadership, but his story includes some surprising episodes that don't fit the usual categories. Perhaps one of the most attractive aspects of his story is that, as so often in the Bible, it is told 'warts and all'!

Bible quotations are taken from the NRSV. Author references are to works in the 'Further reading' list.

# 1 Prayer first

## Nehemiah 1

Reflecting on the nature of intercessory prayer as a call to personal involvement, Metropolitan Anthony writes, 'This is what we truly mean by Intercession. This God… stands at the breaking point of the storm, and he calls us to stand where he stands, to be involved, to be committed… to life and death within the storm' (R. Pooley and P. Seddon, *Lord of the Journey*, p. 231). Nehemiah's story opens with a remarkable and moving example of the kind of prayer that moves into action, intercession worked out in personal commitment.

Holding a privileged post in the court of the Persian king Artaxerxes in Susa, Nehemiah could surely have chosen to remain well clear of the 'trouble and shame' of his fellow Jews, reported to him by his brother Hanani in response to his concerned questions about people and city (vv. 2–3). Scholars continue to debate the chronology of Ezra–Nehemiah, but it seems likely that the bleak news reached Nehemiah in 445BC, a century after Cyrus the Great first encouraged the rebuilding of the Jerusalem temple and 13 years after Ezra's mission (Ezra 7:1–10). Hanani's depressing report may relate to the events of Ezra 4:7–24, when Rehum and other opponents of rebuilding persuaded this same king Artaxerxes to stop the work.

In a situation that demanded urgent *action* (imagine the vulnerability of those broken walls and burned gates), Nehemiah's response of grieving empathy turns into urgent *prayer* – urgent but unhurried, focused by fasting (v. 4) and centred on the theme of repentance. Even more specifically than Ezra (9:5–15), Nehemiah includes himself and his family in anguished confession of his people's failings and the damage they had done to the Lord's concerns. They had all played fast and loose with the God whose fundamental nature is unshakeable love and faithfulness (v. 5).

Repentance is a word of reorientation, of new possibilities. But before looking forward, Nehemiah's prayer looks back at his people's story in the Torah, at God's covenant warnings and promises, given to Moses and repeated by Solomon at the dedication of the temple (vv. 8–10) – the dispersal of unfaithfulness and the homecoming of faithfulness. Boldly, Nehemiah urges God to remember his great work of redemption of his people and their status as his servants (v. 10).

The prayer turns sharply from the realities of the past to the present moment. Only now does the skilled narrator inform us of the special relationship between the king and his courtier and the need for special grace in any possible encounter.

## 2  Prayer now

Nehemiah 2:1–10

Nehemiah's prayer ended on a note of imminent action (1:11). But it seems that he had to wait some four months with the knowledge of damaged Jerusalem and its unhappy inhabitants before the opportunity arose that he prayed for, to raise the issue with the king. Reasons for the delay are unclear; Nehemiah may have been on a rota of cup-bearers or the king may have been away from Susa in one of the other Persian capitals, Ecbatana or Babylon.

During that waiting time, Nehemiah surely prayed often and earnestly, waiting for God's moment. We know from his intercession in chapter 1 that Nehemiah was deeply aware of the Torah's story of his people, but when the king finally asked him what he wanted (v. 4) there was no prescribed script for his response. Nehemiah had to improvise. His arrow prayer at the crucial moment in his dialogue with the king demonstrates his moment-by-moment dependence on God and openness to his Spirit to enable him to respond faithfully. Various factors were in play to cause Nehemiah's fear (v. 2): failure to be cheerful in the king's presence was risky for courtiers; gloom could be interpreted as disloyalty. It's unclear whether Nehemiah's unhappiness was a deliberate ploy to introduce his request or the result of the months of grief and fasting. In addition, it was this king who had put a stop to the rebuilding work in Jerusalem, influenced by the Samaritan faction in Judah (Ezra 4:7–24).

With great wisdom – some would say cunning – Nehemiah, making no mention of Jerusalem, describes his grief and shame that the place of his ancestors' graves lies derelict (v. 3). This was language that all Persians would understand and it prompts the king's question, which is Nehemiah's opportunity: 'What do you request?' Maybe the queen also intervened positively; she is deliberately mentioned (v. 6). Nehemiah has carefully avoided anything that would hint of a bid for political power. The wisdom God gives him prompts a generous response from the king – a passport to Judah and access to building materials from the king's own forest. Not requested but nevertheless provided was an armed guard.

Nehemiah's understanding of the God he served was both intimate ('the gracious hand of my God was upon me', v. 8) and vastly all-encompassing ('I prayed to the God of heaven', v. 4). It was the driving force of his concern for his people, which would now bring him into direct conflict with serious opposition (v. 10).

# 3 Slowly does it

Nehemiah 2:11–20

Some 900 miles separated Susa from Jerusalem. It probably took Nehemiah and his military escort about three months to make the journey – plenty of time for him to continue his dialogue with God and ponder the crucial opening moves in the situation that awaited him in Judah. The opposition of Sanballat and Tobiah was an early warning of hostility to come (vv. 9–10), and even the Jewish population could not be counted on for unified support. We learn later in the story that some of the Jewish elite were doing deals with people like Tobiah (6:17–19). Nehemiah had good reason to prevent news of his plans getting out before he was ready. After a three-day break, secrecy is now the name of the game. Under cover of darkness, with only a few companions – maybe trusted members of his Persian bodyguard – Nehemiah leads a first reconnaissance of Jerusalem's broken fortifications. The narrative is vivid and compelling (vv. 14–15).

Familiarity with scripture can sometimes undermine our sense of the surprising ways in which God works, the unlikely people he chooses for his purposes. Nehemiah had spent his life as a courtier in Persia, trusted as the king's butler, to some extent probably his confidant. As far as we know, nothing prepared him for the task of evaluating the damage to Jerusalem and directing its repair – nothing but the call of God on his life and his practice of utter dependence on the Lord. Scholars tell us that Nehemiah's work was complicated by having to decide which lines the rebuilt walls should follow – those of David's original city or of later expansions (McConville, p. 84).

The surveying work is only part of what faces Nehemiah. When the right moment comes, he must also draw the community together in common enterprise. Armed with the facts, understanding the size of the challenge, he boldly identifies himself with the Jewish remnant and the reputation of God's people: 'You see the trouble we are in… Come, let us rebuild… so that we may no longer suffer disgrace' (v. 17). Together with his account of events back in Susa, Nehemiah's appeal touches hearts and elicits a magnificent and surprising response, given that he is a virtual stranger in Jerusalem: 'They committed themselves to the common good' (v. 18).

No surprise that the commitment to build provokes opposition – Geshem joins the other three in mockery and a repeat accusation of disloyalty to the king. Nehemiah gives them short shrift.

# 4 Leading from the front

Not many people in leadership positions combine single-minded focus on the task with the skills of people management and concern for others. Nehemiah consistently describes himself as a 'servant' rather than a leader (1:6, 11) and maybe it was his style of servant leadership that, according to the testimony of chapter 3, drew together such a varied workforce for this demanding task: priests, goldsmiths, community leaders, women, perfumers and merchants laboured alongside volunteers from places such as Jericho. Forty sections of renewed walls and gates, each with its responsible team, slowly took shape, despite some of the elite who 'would not put their shoulders to the work' (3:5).

This servant leader could also be tough when it came to responding to the taunts of the opposition. He recognised the dangers of discouragement. These days we are all aware of the damaging impact of fake news, the distorted media messages that present a subversive picture of reality. The word from Sanballat and his cronies told a story of hopeless weakness – we can almost hear the scornful laughter of the Samaritan army (vv. 1–3). Nehemiah's response is a fierce prayer-lament, such as we find in Psalm 79, for God's judgement on those who mock God's purposes.

For Nehemiah, leading from the front was becoming increasingly stressful. The community was working well and the project making progress (v. 6). But new allies were joining the enemy – the circle of hostile tribes was closing (vv. 7–8) and there was a real threat of attack. As always in the life of Nehemiah, in crisis, prayer (communal this time) leads to wise action (v. 9). But there is no relief for Nehemiah and his people. Tension builds in the narrative. Maybe the new deployment of guards prompted the problem Judah reports; talk of imminent attack and slaughter was paralysing. Yet again Nehemiah must act strategically and fast, drawing on family allegiances to strengthen defences (v. 13) and reminding his community of their first loyalty and the reason for their confidence: 'Remember the Lord, who is great and awesome' (v. 14).

The tide turns and construction recommences, but the rest of the chapter tells a story of unrelenting pressure on Nehemiah to guide his community into new strategies to face the danger while continuing the building. Throughout the crisis, he is there with them, sharing the hardship and risk (v. 23). There is an unbroken link between Nehemiah's praying and the constant creativity of his strategies. God's Spirit never runs out of ideas!

# 5 The economics of community

After the community's encouraging collaboration in reconstruction and defence, the 'great outcry of the people and of their wives against their Jewish kin' (v. 1) comes as a shock. It is likely that there was a direct link between the successful city reconstruction and the unforeseen economic consequences that prompted the outcry (v. 5). Those goldsmiths, perfumers and merchants whose jobs within the city fed their families had been redeployed to construction work (v. 2). Those who owned and worked land outside Jerusalem had also helped with building; maybe the poorer harvests of the untended fields meant that people had had to mortgage their property to buy food (v. 3). A third group of protestors was struggling to pay the imperial Persian taxes, by mortgaging their land and selling their children as slaves (vv. 4–5).

Unforeseen economic consequences are a sobering aspect of today's pandemic: silent city centres and shuttered shops as people work from home; the dilemma for political leaders of how best to encourage changed behaviour for the common good. No wonder Nehemiah took time, after his initial outrage, to think things over (vv. 6–7a). The Torah did not forbid the mortgaging of property or even the selling of men and women as slaves, but it provides detailed measures against abuse and is marked by a spirit of generosity. Charging of interest was forbidden within the Jewish community and slaves were released after seven years (Deuteronomy 23:19–20; 15:1–18). Nehemiah's response focuses on taking legal measures to stop the profiteering among the financially astute that seems to be part of any human crisis (v. 7). He publicises the charges at a mass meeting. Public shaming has its place in reform (v. 8), but even more important are the practical measures to reverse the damage, to restore to the powerless what is rightly theirs. How refreshing is Nehemiah's refusal of weasel words! 'The thing that you are doing is not good. Should you not walk in the fear of our God?' (v. 9). The nature of the community must reflect the nature of their God: 'Israel was to be a radical challenge to the nations, a specimen of love' (McConville, p. 100).

Nehemiah's personal integrity underpinned his reforms. He didn't say one thing and live another. Verse 10 implies that he and his colleagues had been lending without interest and the closing section of the chapter details his commitment to a generous and non-acquisitive lifestyle as governor in Judah. God's opinion was his deepest concern.

# 6 Intimidation

**Nehemiah 6:1–14**

Reconstruction has continued for almost two months (6:15). The gateways still stand open, waiting for the massive doors to be hung, but otherwise there are no gaps in Jerusalem's wall. Heartening for Nehemiah and his colleagues to watch the progress, but bad news for the rival regional leaders, Sanballat, governor of Samaria, his subordinate Tobiah and their allies, including the Arab chieftain Geshem. They interpreted the reinforcement of the city as the first stage of a bid for renewed political and economic power under Nehemiah's leadership.

The final stages of a demanding project can often be the most challenging. Energy, vision and creativity may all be in short supply. This is a moment of vulnerability, and Nehemiah's opponents are quick to take advantage of a last opportunity to inflict real damage by targeting Nehemiah himself. The pressure builds gradually. Four times his opponents try the softly, softly approach on Nehemiah, proposing a meeting on neutral ground. It was the same kind of hypocritical offer of collaboration that Zerubbabel had rejected during the earlier temple building (Ezra 4:1–3).

Sanballat's fifth communication is much more sinister – a letter deliberately left open so as to encourage rumours of Jewish rebellion and royal ambitions on the part of Nehemiah himself – rumours that will be reported to the Persian king unless Nehemiah agrees to meet his enemies (v. 7). In every case, Nehemiah's response is direct and unambiguous, but another arrow prayer gives us a sense of the spiritual battle in which he is involved (v. 9b).

The insidious nature of the attacks increases in one final strange encounter with a 'prophet'. The open letter had accused Nehemiah of recruiting false prophets in Jerusalem to prophesy in his favour (v. 7). But the one fake prophet identified by Nehemiah turns out to be Sanballat and Tobiah's hired man, instructed to threaten him and lure him inside the temple, forbidden to lay people. There are several puzzling aspects to this episode: why did Nehemiah visit Shemaiah? How did he so quickly understand the truth of the situation? But the strategy rings true: few things undermine the witness of God's people as effectively as getting a public bad name (v. 13). As we shall see in our next reading, Tobiah seems to have been an implacable enemy and was enjoying some success in dividing loyalties within the city (v. 14).

## Guidelines

- The first six chapters of Nehemiah provide a fast-moving narrative that takes him from privileged courtier in Susa to pressured strategist in Judah. Take time to reread the story, including chapter 3, and consider the resources Nehemiah drew on to enable him to improvise faithfully. Do you consider he ever failed to do so?

- Commenting on the economic reforms that Nehemiah introduces in chapter 5, as well as material in Jeremiah 34, Walter Brueggemann writes, 'That is, economic justice is a precondition to secure, viable, humane order in society' (*A Social Reading of the Old Testament*, p. 65). To what extent do you think that the Christian community has been alert enough to economic issues in the pandemic situation and the racial conflicts?

You might like to use this prayer for every day by Bishop Moule (1841):

*Most merciful Saviour, we come to offer you the incense of worshipping hearts. We come as those who by faith behold him who is invisible, we speak to you as simply as if our bodily eyes saw you, as if you were openly seated among us, and your hand was visibly outstretched to give us what we ask... We cannot know what the day will bring, but we know that it will most surely bring your love and grace for your people, and continued opportunities of doing your will and giving ourselves up to your use. Knowing you, we know all we need to know of the unknown future, near or far away... Fill us from within with that holy calm which circumstances can neither give nor take away, for it is yourself dwelling and ruling in us. May we recollect and realise your presence, not at another time only, but today. And in the secret power of it may we meet in peace the common things of life as they come, all calls to act and think for others, all crossings of our will, all pain and joy. Let nothing take us unawares, inasmuch as we are found in you.*

S. Fitzherbert Fox, *A Chain of Prayer across the Ages*, p. 73

# 1 The enemy within

**Nehemiah 6:15—7:4**

The reconstruction of Jerusalem's walls had been carried out and completed in the heat of summer, probably between July and early October 445. As always, Nehemiah attributes this remarkable achievement to God's help, and he perceives a significant shift in how the surrounding nations are viewing events in Jerusalem: their attitude is now characterised by fear and a re-evaluation of their powers, because, Nehemiah believes, they perceive God to be at work (6:16).

At this point in the story, as Nehemiah turns to deal with questions of repopulating the city rather than reconstructing it, he has to cope with another kind of insidious opposition. It becomes evident to him that Tobiah the Ammonite, ally of Sanballat (2:10), is actively forging powerful alliances with some of Judah's elite and almost certainly passing information to Samaria. Indeed some of Tobiah's contacts in Judah were bound to him by marriage (6:18). How hard it must have been for Nehemiah to know where to find solid ground as he read Tobiah's threatening letters while society's influencers, his potential allies and supporters, eagerly extolled Tobiah's virtues and passed on any response Nehemiah might make.

Perhaps surprisingly, in the face of Tobiah's misuse of family relationships, Nehemiah boldly appoints his own brother Hanani to be in charge of the city, alongside Hananiah, a military man who had qualities Nehemiah valued above all in contending with mistrust and unreliability (7:2). Security was understandably a major preoccupation for Nehemiah, especially in the light of the city's sparse population. At this stage Jerusalem seems to have been something of a ghost town. Clearly people were living in Jerusalem and there were houses (7:3). The indication that 'no houses had been built' (7:4) probably means that none had been constructed in the course of repairing the walls or that none had been built into the walls. The appointment of 'the gatekeepers, the singers, and the Levites' (7:1) has puzzled commentators; the singers and Levites were temple staff, not normally appointed to guard duty. Maybe this is another example of Nehemiah's pragmatic and realistic approach, along with his use of lay people as guards – especially when their self-interest could be harnessed (7:3).

# 2 Listening to God together

Nehemiah 7:73—8:12

Johannes Gutenberg's invention of the printing press around the year 1439 brought about momentous change, not least in the way that people engaged with scripture. The Gutenberg Bible in Latin was the first book to be printed, and it opened the door to the privatisation of scripture, to the possibility of personal ownership of a Bible and interpretation of its contents. Things were very different in Bible times. God's story started as oral tradition, told from generation to generation, eventually written down, edited and read aloud in community. Individual reading of scripture was virtually unknown.

This scene, placed by an editor at the heart of Nehemiah's story, provides a fascinating insight into what can happen when a community listens together to God's word. Nehemiah had been working on the repopulation of the city, using the genealogical information of chapter 7 that is the source of the list in Ezra 2. He believed his work was inspired and directed by God in order 'to define the Judean community as a continuation of the pre-exilic people of God, brought through the trauma of exile' (Allen and Laniak, p. 122).

During the pandemic, we have often seen communities celebrating and commemorating. Celebration builds community identity and resilience. The Jewish festival of Trumpets was a minor celebration at the start of the seventh month, a few days after the twenty-fifth of Elul that saw the completion of the city walls – definitely a moment for thanksgiving!

But there is more to this gathering than celebration. The community takes the initiative to ask Ezra to lead a public reading of God's word. Women and men and children old enough to understand stand together for some six hours and listen to Ezra on his wooden pulpit as he reads, probably selectively, from the scroll of the Torah. In doing so, he was obeying God's instruction for the regular public reading of the law, a practice which had probably become neglected in Judah (Deuteronomy 31:9–13). We don't know the significance of the 13 men who stood alongside him – maybe to provide a sense of shared leadership. The group of 13 priests, trained in understanding scripture, circulate through the crowd to listen, comment, explain and maybe translate the Hebrew into Aramaic, 'so that the people understood the reading' (8:8).

With understanding came response: tears of repentance and hope, quiet reflection, shared feasting and a deep sense of the joy of the Lord (8:10).

# 3  The power of remembering

Nehemiah 8:13–18

A vivid memory remains with me of 'scriptural reasoning' sessions – meetings with Jewish and Muslim friends to read our scriptures and listen respectfully to each other's understandings. One meeting coincided with the Jewish feast of Sukkot, also called the feast of Tabernacles or Booths. The liberal Jewish family in whose home we met introduced us to the 'booth' in their garden, where all the family would camp out for seven days. In the 21st century they were remembering and celebrating the 3,000-year-old story of their people's fragile existence in the desert after God freed them from slavery in Egypt.

It seems that the celebration of Sukkot had continued among the exiles (Ezra 3:4–6), but possibly with an emphasis on its nature as a harvest festival (it took place in early autumn). Following the day of public scripture reading, group discussion and teaching, it seems that questions had been raised about how the festival, due in two weeks' time, should most appropriately be celebrated and what its focus should be. Community and faith leaders stayed on after the assembly to meet with Ezra and consider together the relevant scriptures (v. 13). Several Torah texts provided detailed instructions for the festival of Booths. In Numbers, these instructions focus entirely on the daily sacrifices (Numbers 29:12–35). This seems to have provided the model for the festival celebrated after the altar of the temple had been rebuilt in Jerusalem (Ezra 3:4–6). There had been no symbolic booth-building for a long time (v. 17). The instructions recorded in Leviticus (23:39–43) refer to seven days of sacrifices but then describe the celebratory collection of branches and camping out in memory of the ancestors' itinerant existence after the exodus.

Maybe Ezra brought these two key texts together and encouraged discussion of them. Maybe as they looked round at the city's reinforced walls and gates, people reflected on their need to live in conscious dependence on the God who had brought them through the years of wilderness camping. There must be no false trust in the city walls.

It is good to look back from this moment in Nehemiah's story and notice all that has changed since his first bleak survey of the city's crumbling walls. The integrity of the city has been restored, but it's what has happened in the people that is crucial. God's word, proclaimed by faithful people, has moved the community to repentance and transformed behaviour. God's newness is at work. No wonder 'there was very great rejoicing' (v. 17)!

# 4 Iniquities of their ancestors

**Nehemiah 9**

The narrative development of this chapter is puzzling. After the grief prompted by public Torah reading, followed by the joy and celebration of Sukkot, why do the people of Israel turn in the same month to solemn acts of confession, repentance and separation? Some scholars believe this section of the story properly belongs as part of the similar themes in Ezra 9 and 10.

However we understand the sequence, what impresses and moves us here is the continuing centrality of the communal listening to the word of God and its power to inform prayer and to move people to confession and worship. This is Hebrews 4:12 coming alive before our eyes: the living and active word, sharper than any sword, judging the thoughts and intentions of the heart. In our church practice, to what extent do we give priority to hearing God's word in ways that enable his people truly to enter the story and find their place in it, the story that tells us who we are? So often our public Bible readings are brief and contextless.

At the time of writing these reflections, alongside the distress caused by the pandemic, western societies have also been confronting, or refusing to confront, the same issue as the people of Israel, 'the iniquities of their ancestors' (v. 2). We live today, as all people live, with the outcomes of the sinful choices of previous generations, as well as our own. It's been a shock to be confronted, for example, with the statistics of the wealth of the UK slave trade or the breathtaking amounts of corrupt finance processed today in the London markets.

Ezra's public prayer of confession is a recital of the entire story of God's people from Genesis creation to their present enslavement under alien powers in the promised land (vv. 6, 36–37). The prayer moves constantly between the evidence of God's patience, mercy and fidelity and the people's repeated faithlessness. The God honoured in this prayer is creator, sovereign, one who sees and hears his people, patient guide and sustainer, and one who deals justly with his fickle and rebellious people. We can surely imagine the listening community responding throughout: indrawn breath, weeping, murmurs of joy. The long story of God's dealings is hopeful, but his people must take seriously the implications of their identity. The time had come for a renewal of the covenant promises of love and loyalty, a solemn, documented commitment to live differently (10:29).

# 5  Joy in Jerusalem

**Nehemiah 12:27–47**

Celebration has already been a vital part of the community's responses to the process of restoration, both of the city and of the people (8:12). The ceremonies that mark the dedication of the rebuilt city walls mark the culmination of Nehemiah's two-stage mission and parallel the completion of the temple at the end of Ezra's first mission (Ezra 6:16–18).

The community that now celebrates has a different feel about it. Chapter 11 describes a programme to increase the population of Jerusalem beyond those who had returned from exile, listed in chapter 7. The new system provided for every tenth person to live within the city while nine remained in the outlying towns (11:25–36). Some of the new Jerusalem citizens were volunteers, others the result of drawing lots to avoid all appearance of favouritism. It seems that, for reasons that are unclear, people viewed living in Jerusalem as a matter of sacrifice; their fellow citizens appreciated their willingness to do so (11:1–2).

Exuberant joy is the keynote of the dedication ceremonies. Nehemiah uses the word five times in verse 43! Two 'great companies' of worship leaders and musicians, reinforced by recruits from outside the city, proceed in opposite directions around the walls towards the east side of the city, to meet at the temple (v. 40). We can only imagine Nehemiah's emotions as he walked with one group and surely remembered that depressing night-time ride round the ruined walls months earlier and the taunts of Tobiah (4:3).

There is a strong sense of continuity and of 'normal service resumed' in the closing verses (vv. 44–47).

# 6  Authentic reform?

We instinctively want Nehemiah's story to end with 'the joy of Jerusalem' (12:43) as the climax of the successful restoration of both city and people. But the editor of this text had other ideas and provides a narrative that is difficult to follow in chronological terms: 'There is an audacious clash between the literary composition and the historical timetable in the interests of a spiritual lesson' (Allen and Laniak, p. 159). That lesson is that worship is not an end in itself; it must be worked out in lives of integrity, in community lifestyle that reflects the character of God.

'On that day' (12:44; 13:1) almost certainly refers to the events of chapter 10, when the covenant provisions were agreed and signed after the communal listening to God's word. The reforms that result range from proper provision for the temple staff to exclusion from temple worship of all who were not of Israelite descent – less drastic action than the wholesale divorces under Ezra of 13 years earlier (Ezra 10), but a sign that inter-tribal alliances were still a problem.

'Now, before this...' (v. 4) opens a diverse and disturbing closing section of Nehemiah's story. Once again scholars differ on their understanding of the chronology, especially the timing of Nehemiah's return to Persia and back to Judah (v. 6). One likely scenario sees Nehemiah back in the Persian court after overseeing the covenant agreement and repopulation of the city. News of Eliashib's treacherous and nepotistic behaviour must have reached him there and prompted him to ask the king for permission to return to Judah to clean up the situation, rid the temple of his old foe Tobiah and appoint faithful new staff. The other lapses that Nehemiah had to deal with on his return were sadly familiar. People were being careless about keeping the sabbath (vv. 15–22), influenced by the practices of outsiders (v. 16) and, most disturbing of all to Nehemiah, the mixed marriages continued (v. 25), the worst case being the alliance between the high priest's son and Sanballat's daughter (v. 28).

Nehemiah's prayers continue as part of the record (vv. 14, 22, 31). 'Remember me, O my God,' he pleads, as his reforming work appears to be unravelling and the story that unfolds in Ezra and Nehemiah closes on a note of ambiguity. McConville (p. 149) notes a sense of desperation and weariness in Nehemiah as he faces the tenuous nature of his community's commitment to the Lord.

# Guidelines

- The second half of the book of Nehemiah focuses on opposition and on reform and return to covenant living. Nehemiah describes himself as a 'servant of God': how would you evaluate his response to opposition and his approach to reform? To what extent is he a model for church leadership today?

- 'The returning exiles under Ezra and Nehemiah were a people with memory and hope… That was what enabled them to survive and continue as the people participating in the long-term mission of God for the nations… The challenge for today's church is to recognise that a significant factor in the loss of missional effectiveness is our loss of biblical memory and hope… We fail to live in, by, and for the biblical story we are part of' (Shepherd and Wright, p. 169). What is your experience of scripture engagement in your Christian community? What might helpfully be done differently?

- The issue of repentance for the sins of previous generations is complex. To what extent might Nehemiah's story have changed your perspective?

**FURTHER READING**

Leslie C. Allen and Timothy S. Laniak, *Ezra, Nehemiah, Esther* (Hendrickson Publishers, 2003).

John Goldingay, *Ezra, Nehemiah and Esther for Everyone* (SPCK, 2012).

J.G. McConville, *Ezra, Nehemiah, and Esther* (Westminster John Knox Press, 1985).

David J. Shepherd and Christopher J.H. Wright, *Ezra and Nehemiah* (Eerdmans, 2018).

Joseph Too Shao and Rosa Ching Shao, *Ezra and Nehemiah: A pastoral and contextual commentary* (Langham Partnership, 2019).

# Mark 14—16: facing the cross

Steve Motyer

Welcome back to Mark – to our last visit, which will take us through his so-called passion narrative, the events of the last five days of Jesus' story: two of which he spends in the grave.

It's a powerfully told story, put together by a master storyteller, who sets us off on the right track at the end of chapter 13 by telling us to 'Watch!' (13:37). That call by Jesus to his disciples to stay alert, to watch out, matches the position of the women in 15:40 who are 'watching' Jesus die and note the place of his burial (15:47). We are in that position as readers of this story, watching, noting, trying to see what is really happening. And, as we'll notice, Mark keeps helping us to see below the surface of the story, in particular to be aware of what *God* is doing as a hidden actor directing these events and doing something completely out of the awareness of the main human actors.

The subtle fulfilment of scripture is especially significant in giving this deeper perspective, as we'll see. This is important because of the terrible shame and degradation which was attached to crucifixion. The natural assumption of nearly all readers – unlike the centurion in 15:39 – would have been that anyone who died in this way was condemned by *God* as well as by Rome and by the Jewish authorities. How could such a figure be God's Messiah? Mark wants to show that Jesus dies as 'a ransom for many' (10:45), and that his death is therefore the greatest good news and the heart of *God's* action to save the world – the beginning of a worldwide proclamation centred on the message of the cross (see 14:9).

Unless otherwise stated, Bible quotations are my own translation. Author references are to works in the 'Further reading' list.

# 1  Anointed for burial

**Mark 14:1–11**

We begin the passion story as we might expect – with the plot to kill Jesus (vv. 1–2). Actually, we meet one of Mark's clever 'sandwich' narratives here, for verses 1–2 (which pose the question – how can we kill him quietly?) are balanced by verses 10–11 (which provide the answer – ah, that's how: through betrayal by one of his disciples).

As with all Mark's sandwich stories, this horrifying, cynical framework gives the angle from which to read the story in the middle. In contrast to Judas, who is willing to *take* money to betray Jesus (v. 11), we meet an unnamed woman who is willing to *give* extravagantly to him. The alabaster jar, worth a year's wages (v. 5) and containing perfumed oil (possibly derived from pistachio nuts), was probably a family heirloom, kept for a rainy day, or maybe it was her dowry. It was an extremely valuable possession, which she is willing to spend completely on Jesus. Whether or not it was intended as Jesus interprets it (v. 8), this amazing action anticipates what a group of women will attempt to do at the other end of the passion story (see 16:1). It is one of the great ironies of the story – pointing to the way in which death is reversed here – that Jesus' body is anointed for burial before he dies, and not after.

Some of the disciples disapprove of this 'waste' (v. 4). Though dressed up as concern for the poor (v. 5), their comments implicitly show how they value Jesus; they would not think of giving him something as costly as this. Perhaps it's not surprising that, before long, they will desert him and run away (14:50).

Jesus commends her action in the warmest possible way: 'Truly I tell you, wherever the gospel is preached in all the world, what this woman has done will be spoken of, in memory of her' (v. 9). And here's another wonderful irony. The next incident we meet is the story of the last supper, the Passover meal which Jesus transforms into a memorial meal for himself. But Mark doesn't actually use the language of 'remembrance' in his account of the last supper, even though we know how important this was (see Luke 22:19; 1 Corinthians 11:24–25). In Mark, that language is reserved for this woman – *she* will be remembered, standing for all who are willing to 'remember' Jesus as she does here.

# 2  Setting the stage

This is one of those biblical stories which makes us ask, 'Why is it here?' The same applies to the very similar story in 11:1–7, with which the last section of Mark began. Again, two disciples are sent on a special quest based on Jesus' prophetic awareness. In both cases, why does Mark want us to know about these preparatory moves, to provide (a) a donkey for Jesus to ride into Jerusalem, and (b) a room for his Passover meal there?

Behind Jesus' prophetic awareness lies God's superintendent organising of the situation – providing a donkey waiting patiently in the street (and not working in the fields at that moment) and an unbooked room in Jerusalem at the last minute, on the very day of the Passover meal. Jerusalem was completely packed with Passover visitors each year, because Passover could only be celebrated there, and so all available accommodation was usually taken well in advance. Remarkably, the disciples find a room which is large, available and prepared for a meal involving both a rabbi and his followers (v. 14)!

Mark is saying: when we are walking in the flow of God's will, on his 'way' (compare 10:32, 52), then doors open and what we need is provided, even if we have to stick our necks out with impertinent faith in responding to the leading of his Spirit. The relationship between Jesus and his Father is underlined, because Jesus knows what to look for and God has the provision all lined up.

There's more. In both cases (though in different ways) the fulfilment of scripture is what motivates God's wonderful provision. In 11:1–7, the provision of the donkey enables a subtly staged fulfilment of Zechariah 9:9 (though Mark leaves us, his readers, to spot this). Here in chapter 14, the provision of the Passover room indicates how important it is in God's eyes that Jesus shows his disciples – and us – how the meaning of the Passover is caught up and taken further through his death on the cross (as we will see tomorrow). So as we struggle through the thronged streets of Jerusalem with these two puzzled disciples, and spot the man with the water jar, and follow him, and then discover the upper room already prepared, we know that something very special is in store at this Passover meal.

As we will see, this notion of God's secret superintendence is vital for the whole passion.

# 3 Poured out

**Mark 14:17–31**

We will take two days over this passage, which is of such significance to Christians, as it contains the institution of the Eucharist, our central act of worship.

Jesus' words and actions instituting the Eucharist (vv. 22–25) are actually the heart of another Markan sandwich. Verses 17–21 and 26–31 balance each other – the former focusing on the announcement of Jesus' betrayal by 'one of you', and the latter on the announcement of Jesus' abandonment by all the disciples, and of Peter's denial in particular. In both paragraphs there is horrified questioning and rejection of the idea – 'Surely not I!' they all say to each other (v. 19), and with Peter they all say, 'Even if I must die with you, I will never deny you!' (v. 31).

The irony is so huge. We know the truth: Jesus will be betrayed, they will all desert him and Peter will deny him three times. Sandwiched into this crackling atmosphere of grief, horror, indignation, puzzlement and extravagant assertion of loyalty – and against the background of Jesus' certainty that their commitment is empty – he speaks the glorious words of institution, which also point ahead to the terrible events of the coming night. But view them from an entirely different perspective: Jesus will die, but not because one of his disciples betrays him and the rest abandon and deny him; rather, because he will give his body and blood to establish the covenant between God and his people (v. 24). At the very moment when they abandon their loyalty to him – and through the very same action of betrayal – Jesus acts to re-establish God's loyal covenant commitment to them and to all his people.

There is such 'Amazing Grace' here. By sandwiching the story in this way, Mark brings the action of the cross into the closest possible connection with our human sinfulness, frailty and pride. The betrayal and the denial are terrible – 'it would have been good if that man had never been born' (v. 21), rather than live to do such a dreadful thing. But how amazing it is, that human sinfulness and betrayal become the occasion, even the *channel*, through which God delivers salvation to his rebellious people – people like us. Into this darkest of moments comes the glorious invitation, 'Take, this is my body… this is my blood of the covenant, poured out for many' (vv. 22–23).

**20–26 September**

25

# 4 As it has been written

As we continue to look at these few verses, we note that Mark's two outer sandwich sections are also united by reference to the fulfilment of scripture. Jesus says, 'For the Son of Man goes as it has been written about him, but woe to that man through whom the Son of Man is betrayed' (v. 21) – and then he later tells the disciples, 'You will all stumble and fall, for it is written, "I will strike the shepherd, and the sheep will be scattered"' (v. 27, quoting Zechariah 13:7). Scripture will be fulfilled both by Judas' betrayal of Jesus and by the disciples' desertion of him.

This emphasis reflects the way in which the Passover meal is itself picked up and 'fulfilled' in the central section. Jesus invests the bread and the cup of the Passover with new meaning – with reference to himself. The Passover is a vivid annual memorial of Israel's deliverance from Egypt, with the story retold and the elements of the meal re-enacting the night of the exodus. But Jesus refocuses the meal on himself – even more clearly in the other accounts, with the words 'Do this in remembrance of *me*' (Luke 22:19; 1 Corinthians 11:24). The exodus has been displaced in favour of an even greater memorial.

It could be that this emphasis on the fulfilment of scripture (a feature of the whole passion story) was motivated by a desire to prove to Jewish sceptics that this most unlikely event, the crucifixion of the Messiah, really was God's plan: he was in it, and behind it! Even Jesus' betrayal and abandonment by his disciples fulfilled scriptural expectation.

But does that not undermine their responsibility for their action, if they *had* to betray him in order to fulfil scripture? James Edwards comments that verse 21 'is one of the most suggestive verses in scripture on the relationship between divine causality and human responsibility' (Edwards, p. 424). And what it suggests is that God can 'superintend' events so that our actions are both fully our own and 'meant' by him as part of a bigger purpose to bring about his goals. 'God meant it for good,' said Joseph to his brothers, with reference to their cruel action in selling him into slavery (Genesis 50:20) – a 'meaning for good' that can touch even the most ghastly events with a hidden purpose of love: even terrible betrayal, even the crucifixion of the Son of God.

# 5 The agony of waiting

**Mark 14:32–36**

The Passover meal ended, Jesus and his disciples go to a favourite spot, a garden on the Mount of Olives: so favourite, in fact, that Jesus knows Judas will seek him there (see John 18:2; Luke 22:39). He is deliberately waiting for the temple police and the arrest.

As he waits, he prays. But fascinatingly, he does not want to pray alone. He wants the company of the very people whom he knows will desert him and flee when the arresting party arrives. Peter's coming denial does not seem to count against Jesus' valuing of him as a friend who can stand alongside him in this agony of waiting.

We know that Peter was a particular source for Mark's gospel, so it was probably from Peter that Mark learned of Jesus' sudden distress ('deeply distressed and troubled', v. 33; 'my soul is overwhelmed with grief, like I'm pressed down into death', v. 34). Peter must have heard the agonised prayer in verses 35–36, shortly before drifting off to sleep.

The ancient world's wise men were admired for facing death with equanimity. The Greek philosopher Socrates is the most famous example: Plato describes how, about to be executed by poison, Socrates gladly welcomed death as the soul's friend, because his soul was about to be released from the body into true immortality. Some early Christians felt embarrassed that Jesus was not like that. Why was he not? Even more, why did Peter, James and John not 'hush up' this display of weakness, but make sure that it was recorded?

There are two factors here – first the manner, but more simply just the fact, of Jesus' coming death. Death by crucifixion was 'the most cruel and disgusting punishment' in the Romans' arsenal of devices of torture (Cicero's description). It was a horrendous way to die. Jesus quails before it. But more than the terrible suffering, death is not a door to freedom in biblical thought. Far from it. It is 'the last enemy' (1 Corinthians 15:26), an assault on the person which results in the total destruction of each human being. Apart from God's specific preservation or rescue, death is the end of us.

So Jesus fears and shuns it – and yet submits to it, in obedience to his Father's will (v. 36). The author of Hebrews, meditating on this Gethsemane story, sees Jesus' tears and prayers and submission to God's will as the heart of his atoning sacrifice (Hebrews 5:7–10).

**20–26 September**

27

# 6 Speaking of human weakness

It is wonderful that Jesus' weakness in the face of death is matched in this story by the disciples' parallel weakness – in the face of sleep. Natural human weakness is written all over here – that kind of weakness which goes with the territory of being human, but which still may mean that we mess up, let each other down and fail God's call on our lives. The difference is that Jesus arms himself with a passionate embracing of God's will for him (14:36), while the three apostles have not only forgotten Jesus' words in 13:35–37, but also – in Peter's case – are sleeping on the job of living up to his passionate commitment made just a few minutes earlier (14:31).

What does it mean to 'deny' Jesus? Three times Jesus comes back and finds them sleeping (v. 41), and a first-time reader of Mark (not aware of what happens next) might well wonder whether this failure to 'watch' with Jesus is the fulfilment of his prediction that Peter will deny him three times (v. 30). It's a repeated denial of companionship at a time of great need.

Jesus' words in verse 38 are his reply to Peter's passionate profession of absolute discipleship in verse 31. 'Okay, Peter – but you won't be able to carry that through unless you "keep watch, and pray that you will not come into testing. The spirit is willing, but the flesh is weak!"' Jesus echoes the words of the Lord's Prayer here, 'Lead us not into testing / temptation' (Matthew 6:13) – which is a prayer recognising that God *does* sometimes lead us into trial and testing (like Abraham and Job), and that such times are awful, dangerous and to be avoided if at all possible. Hence the prayer. Jesus has just prayed this prayer himself (14:36), but he knows that the 'trial' is coming, nonetheless. He wants Peter (in fact, all of them: verse 38 is addressed to 'you' plural) to pray the same prayer, so that their bravado will never actually be put to the test.

This is about facing our human weakness, not denying it or ignoring it. It is about recognising that sometimes life will thrust us into situations where we simply cannot cope, and that in those situations our acceptance of our weakness will become the point at which God's strength can become very real for us (compare 2 Corinthians 12:9). Jesus is about to prove the truth of this!

# Guidelines

The cross is looming. What has stood out for you this week, as we have begun to read Mark's passion narrative together?

For me, there is something powerful and wonderful about the way in which God's plan is fulfilled through human actors of all sorts: the rebellious and treacherous, the weak and defiant, the puzzled and offended, the ignorant, the opinionated, the loving, the passionate and the sleepy… All human life is here, and of course at the heart of it all there is one who is as weak as all of us in the face of death, but who knows that God will give him the strength to bear what he must, even though he feels completely terrified.

The human motives and actions matter – it makes a great difference how people behave. But through it all (underlined by the repeated idea that scripture is being fulfilled at point after point), God's purpose is being fulfilled. This story is going somewhere very special – as we see from the passing reference to the worldwide preaching of the gospel in the story of the alabaster jar (14:9) and the way in which *this* Passover meal points forward to the final messianic banquet in heaven, when Jesus will once again feast with his disciples (14:25). Messy it may be, but glory is definitely coming.

The same is surely true for us! Whatever weakness and suffering we endure – our own and others' – God's purpose is for life and salvation, and he will bring us through.

# 1 'Rise, let's go!'

With these words in verse 42, Jesus signals the appearance of the arresting squad and summons the sleeping disciples to their feet. But interestingly, 'let us go' keeps the initiative with Jesus, even though the word 'seize' is used three times in these verses to describe what the squad does to Jesus (vv. 44, 46, 49 – and again in v. 51 of the young man who struggles out of his onesie and escapes). This armed force comes expecting Jesus' followers to resist, and indeed one of them has a go (v. 47), but basically Jesus actively surrenders to the arrest, submitting to Judas' flamboyant 'kiss' and knowing what it really means. This is about rising and going to do his Father's will.

The control is also taken away from the arresting band by Jesus' reference to the fulfilment of scripture (v. 49). He points out that they could have arrested him at any time while teaching in the temple – why did they delay? 'So that the scriptures might be fulfilled,' he suggests. But that was *not* why they didn't arrest him earlier – we heard the reason for this in 14:2, when the Sanhedrin decided, 'Not during the festival, for the people will surely riot.' Once again we see, behind and through all the human machinations and scheming, the hidden purpose of God who – well, what exactly does he do? Again we bump into the mysterious interweaving of divine and human agency, in which both are fully operative. The arrest was delayed, so that scripture might be fulfilled.

And irony of ironies – what a scripture. Taking place in this way – in the middle of the night, in this secret garden, rather than during the day surrounded by crowds in the temple – the arrest gives the disciples full opportunity to forsake Jesus and flee (v. 50): no ifs or buts or fudges. The scripture in question here is Zechariah 13:7, quoted in verse 27 and now fulfilled in glorious technicolour. The little story in verses 51–52 – only in Mark's gospel – underlines the energy with which the disciples fled and also hints at another scripture, Amos' vision of the coming day of judgement when 'even the bravest warriors will flee naked' (Amos 2:16, NIV). So beyond the awfulness of the betrayal and the abandonment, we see what scripture calls 'God's hand' at work – and surely Jesus took comfort in this. He goes forward in his Father's will, into the horror ahead.

# 2 The sheep before his shearers

Mark does love the sandwich technique! Here's another one: two paragraphs about Peter (vv. 53–54 and 66–72) bracket the story of Jesus' trial before the Sanhedrin in Caiaphas' villa (vv. 55–65). The key theme that holds the sandwich together is witness: the contrast between false and failed witness, on the one hand (Peter's denial and the false witnesses in verses 56–59), and the bold, clear witness of Jesus to his true identity in verse 62, on the other. Once again Jesus' commitment to *be who he is* shines out in a deeply alien context that seeks to deny him completely.

Jesus is brought before a highly irregular night-time gathering of the Sanhedrin in the High Priest's private mansion. Peter follows 'at a distance' (v. 54) and sits with 'the servants' in the open courtyard below the room where Jesus is being tried. Mark is clear that the Sanhedrin simply wants rid of Jesus and is looking for an accusation that will give his execution credibility (v. 55). The accusers in verses 56–59 are therefore probably members of the Sanhedrin, rather than external 'witnesses'.

They try hard to make a capital charge stick. But the best they can manage is a garbled version of Mark 13:2, perhaps with 13:26 and 8:31 thrown in. Interestingly, in John 2:19 Jesus says something much closer to the accusation here, though not that *he* will destroy the temple. It would indeed have been a serious matter, if Jesus had threatened to destroy the temple himself, and the charge that he said this was thrown later at Stephen (Acts 6:14). Here, Jesus makes no attempt to refute the charge – but even so his accusers can't make it stick (v. 59). We must imagine that there are some secret supporters of Jesus in the Sanhedrin who probe these 'witnesses' and are easily able to undermine their false testimony (we meet one later – see Mark 15:43; compare John 7:50–51).

So it is a significant moment when the High Priest rises to his feet to take charge of this search for a capital accusation (v. 60). He first tries to make something of Jesus' silence – is it acquiescence in these charges? Far from it. Mark's readers know that this is the mark of Isaiah's 'servant of the Lord' – 'Like a sheep that before its shearers is silent, so he did not open his mouth' (Isaiah 53:7, NRSV).

But his silence is about to end!

# 3 The court that matters

Finally, in response to the High Priest's direct question (v. 61), Jesus breaks his silence. Once again, he takes the proceedings into his own hands, because his words break the impasse in the Sanhedrin and 'enable' the High Priest to pronounce, 'Blasphemy! Deserving death!' (v. 64). That is where Jesus knows that it must go, within the will of his Father.

There is a wonderful irony here, because the High Priest's words requires inflexion to *make* them a question. By themselves, they are a statement – indeed, a confession of faith: 'You are the Christ, the Son of the Blessed One!' But the High Priest is asking, not confessing, and he elicits a powerful response from Jesus: 'I am! And you [plural] will see the Son of Man seated at the right hand of the Power, and coming with the clouds of heaven' (v. 62).

To dig into this amazing response, we must bear in mind an essential piece of temple theology believed by the High Priest and indeed the whole Sanhedrin: namely that the earthly temple derives its vital status and importance from the fact that it mirrors and represents the heavenly sanctuary where God dwells, surrounded by angels. Jesus plugs into this theology when he recasts the High Priest's description of him in terms drawn from Daniel 7:13, the verse on which he also drew in 13:26, at the climax of his apocalyptic teaching about the destruction of the temple. Daniel's vision is of an amazing scene taking place in the *heavenly* sanctuary – the investment of 'one like a son of man' with kingship, power and glory as he approaches God's throne riding on the clouds of heaven. As 'the Christ, the Son of the Blessed One,' Jesus is this glorious 'Son of Man'.

So Jesus is not ignoring the false testimony against him, but making a claim much more dramatic, and disturbing, than merely destroying or rebuilding the earthly temple. Far more significant is what will happen in the temple 'not made with hands' (v. 58) – the heavenly one, the only court whose judgement finally matters. In that court, he is truly the King.

So now, with condemnation, shame, terrible suffering and death looming before this 'Son of Man', the moment has come for Jesus to break his silence. In fact, his words precipitate all the dreadful things about to unfold, which begin immediately with mockery and blows (v. 65).

# 4 Peter's denial

This is an incredibly sad, but also strangely hopeful, passage. It's amazing that Peter's denials of Jesus are highlighted to this extent. Peter was so important in the early church, and yet not only is his action not covered up, but also each of the three denials is described in horrible detail. We even hear that he called down divine curses to emphasise, 'I don't know this person of whom you speak!' (v. 71). And it is not a squad of soldiers that intimidates him, but a single servant girl who 'looks at' him (v. 67) – Mark uses the same word that described how Jesus 'looked at' the young man in 10:21. She, too, 'looks' with insight, but Peter doesn't want to be seen. Even the reference to Peter being 'Galilean' (v. 70) underlines the awfulness of his action, for Galilee was the scene of Peter's spiritual triumphs – performing miracles and preaching in Jesus' name (Mark 6:7–13), and even (further north, in Caesarea Philippi) being the first disciple to confess what Jesus has just boldly acknowledged before the High Priest (Mark 8:29; 14:61–62).

Why is this passage here? In a way, that seeing is the clue. The Sanhedrin members who mock Jesus command him to 'prophesy!' (v. 65), wanting mockingly to prove that he can't. But at that very moment, downstairs in the courtyard, his prophecy about Peter is being fulfilled. Jesus could truly see Peter and knew where his loud protestations would end up (14:31) – a seeing mirrored now in the accusatory eyes of the servant girl. But we know what Jesus does when he sees people in all their pride, weakness and false security: he loves them (10:21). He is giving his life for such people.

This is what makes it possible for the sin to be seen by us, in all its awfulness. Mark doesn't spare the details of Peter's failure, because *Jesus* sees it: after the third denial Luke includes the further detail that 'the Lord turned and looked at Peter', using the same verb (Luke 22:61). He sees Peter's sin fully, in all its fear, pain and betrayal, and that means that, finally, *it doesn't matter*. It's covered.

This is such a powerful message. Maybe it would be appropriate today to allow yourself to know that the sins that bother you (whether yours or the sins of others) are truly seen and known by Christ, and are not beyond his capacity to cover.

# 5 Before Pilate

The story moves on. Verse 1 is puzzling, because we thought that the Sanhedrin was already sitting and had just reached its verdict about Jesus (14:64). The Greek could mean 'reached a decision' rather than 'held a meeting' (so NIV) – or maybe Mark means us to understand that the Sanhedrin broke up briefly and convened again in the early morning in their usual hall beside the temple, rather than in the High Priest's residence. Either way, they decide to send Jesus to the Roman governor, Pontius Pilate.

The background to this is probably the restriction placed on Jewish power by the Romans, that officially they could not carry out capital punishments (see John 18:31). This did not stop them stoning people to death when enraged (see Acts 7:54-60), but on this occasion they decide against mob justice and try to enlist the governor.

Pilate's question to Jesus ('Are you the King of the Jews?', v. 2a) is like the High Priest's (14:61) – it is phrased as a statement which becomes a question only with voice inflexion. Later, nailed over Jesus' head on the cross (15:26), it is indeed a statement, but one whose meaning is in the eye of the beholder – a source of ridicule (15:32) or a prompt to real faith (15:39). This helps us to understand Jesus' response here (v. 2b): 'you say' (literally) could also be inflected as a question, 'Do *you* say that?' So we could paraphrase it, 'That's down to you to decide!' Jesus' kingship is always one which has to be recognised and acknowledged – unlike Roman rule, it is never imposed by force. Will Pilate acknowledge that Jesus is 'king of the Jews'?

This title appears without prior notice. Clearly the leaders of the Sanhedrin have invented it as a way of making Jesus appear politically subversive to the Romans. Jesus has actually proclaimed the kingdom of *God*, not his own (Mark 1:15). But it is not inappropriate, granted Daniel's vision of the power and 'kingship' bestowed on the 'Son of Man' (Daniel 7:14). So once again the initiative shifts to Jesus, because it becomes a live question: is the Sanhedrin doing this to one who is *truly* their 'king'?

So Jesus' 'You say!' jumps off the page and addresses every reader of Mark, too – not just Pilate. Whether Jewish or Gentile, Mark's readers have to take sides: guilty or innocent? Blasphemer or truly king? It's down to each to decide!

# 6 Pilate's decision

**Mark 15:6–15**

Which way will Pilate jump in response to Jesus' challenging reply in verse 2? Will he acknowledge him as 'king of the Jews' or not? Mark keeps this teasingly open, as he shows Pilate trying three times to release Jesus in line with the custom that a prisoner is released at every Passover (v. 6). Verses 6–8 set the scene, leading to Pilate's first attempt: to 'the crowd' that has appeared to ask for this custom to be honoured, he says, 'Do you want me to release the king of the Jews for you?' (v. 9)

Does this mean he really thinks Jesus could be 'the king of the Jews'? Or is he just being cynical, teasing the crowd with the title the chief priests have used as an accusation? Mark's comment in verse 10 just deepens the uncertainty: 'For he realised that the chief priests had handed him over because of jealousy.' In other words, he knows that Jesus is no political threat to Rome; he is only before Pilate because the chief priests hate and fear him. But what does he think about this title? The chief priests spur the crowd to cry for the release of a prisoner who certainly is a political threat to Rome (v. 11). Will Pilate agree?

Pilate's second question (v. 12) deepens the mystery. 'What then do you want me to do to [the one you call] the King of the Jews?' The phrase in brackets ('the one you call') is not in some of the most significant and early texts of Mark – and it could well have been slipped in by scribes who were influenced by Matthew 27:22 and who wanted to make it clear that Pilate did *not* accept this title of Jesus. Without it, Pilate's challenge is all the sharper: what do they want to happen to their king? Their answer is clear and cruel (v. 13).

Pilate's third question reveals that at least he believes firmly in Jesus' innocence (v. 14). But now we see his true colours. Sources outside the New Testament show that Pilate despised the Jews and could act with great cynicism and cruelty towards them. But appeasing the local population is worth a lot (v. 15a), so he releases a known terrorist and has an innocent man flogged – a simply terrible punishment that often led to the death of its victims – before handing him over for crucifixion.

# Guidelines

Once again, it is worth asking what stands out and speaks to you particularly from this week's readings.

As I have been writing these notes, I could not help remembering the experience of watching Mel Gibson's powerful film *The Passion of the Christ* (2004). For me – as I guess for many – the scene that really stood out and remains in memory is the flogging at the pillar, a gruesome and realistic (and historically well-based) depiction of the part of the story that Mark covers with just one word in 15:15, *fragellosas*, 'having flogged him'. Unlike the film, Mark is very restrained in the actual depiction of Jesus' sufferings, but he leaves us in no doubt about the awfulness of what Jesus endured, in all its dimensions (not just the physical torture).

And that leaves me with a deep sense of the sheer courage with which Jesus faced all this – the injustice, the hatred, the betrayal, the isolation, the mockery and the torture. According to theologian and philosopher Paul Tillich, courage is not just one 'virtue' alongside others like love and kindness, but is basic to being human – a quality essential for human life itself, because only courage, based in faith, can face the fear prompted by the three terrible threats of death, meaninglessness and condemnation. Jesus' courageous 'self-affirmation' (to use Tillich's word) is so beautifully and powerfully expressed in his amazing words in 14:62: this is what sustains him as his disciples desert him and both Jews and Romans threaten him with death, curse him and condemn him.

May God likewise give us 'the courage to be' (the title of Tillich's book) as we too face these threats in the unique form in which we each experience them.

# 1 Crucified

**Mark 15:16–24**

This brief passage takes us from Pilate's decision in verse 15 to its execution in verse 24, 'and they crucified him'. Mark tells it in such simple, direct language, each word adding its own colour to a very vivid picture of Jesus' journey from Pilate's presence, through the large open court of Herod's magnificent palace (v. 15) and then along what we now call the Via Dolorosa through Jerusalem to Golgotha, the place of crucifixion, just outside the city walls (v. 22).

Mark clearly does not want us to dwell on Jesus' physical torment and pain. He highlights instead first the mockery of the Roman garrison – ironically offering him the worship he truly deserves (vv. 18–19) – and then their press-ganging of Simon to carry Jesus' cross, because presumably Jesus was so weakened by the flogging (v. 15) that he could not carry it himself. Finally, Mark highlights the events around the crucifixion – the offering of wine, which Jesus refuses (v. 23), and the division of his clothes among the soldiers (v. 24).

Does Mark have an agenda in telling the story in this way? He certainly has an eye for the symbolic. Not only do the soldiers horribly symbolise true worship, but also Simon symbolises discipleship for us, taking up the cross behind Jesus as he said (Mark 8:34). And it could be that Mark mentions 'Alexander and Rufus' (v. 21) because they were disciples known to his readers, also on the Way behind Jesus (see Romans 16:13 – very possibly the same Rufus). These events also have a deeper meaning as fulfilments of prophecy, pointing to God's purpose being fulfilled even in this terrible sequence. He is in charge! Thus the mockery, spitting, scourging and finally killing are exactly as Jesus himself predicted in 10:33–34 – and in addition the mockery recalls the messianic sufferings described in Psalm 22:7–8 and Isaiah 50:6. The offering of the wine recalls Psalm 69:21 (another psalm regarded as messianic in the New Testament), and the division of the clothes points to Psalm 22:18 – in fact, Mark's words in verse 24 are a direct echo of the language of that verse.

Crucifixion was deliberately a deeply shaming and excessively cruel form of execution. For this reason, it was extremely hard for many to accept that this mocked and shamed figure could be God's Messiah. But for Mark, that is the glorious heart of the good news, signalled by these pointed fulfilments of scripture.

# 2  The mockery goes on

Mark continues to highlight the mockery heaped on Jesus as he hangs on the cross: we now hear insults from the passers-by (v. 29), the chief priests and scribes (v. 31) and even the two crucified with him (v. 32b). Why does Mark have this emphasis in telling the story of the crucifixion? He lived in an environment in which, as Paul puts it in 1 Corinthians 1:23, the story of the cross was 'a stumbling-block to Jews and folly to the Gentiles' – in other words, the mockery carried on. Jews could not understand how anyone could see this shamed, condemned figure as the Messiah: did not the manner of his death show what God thought of him? And for non-Jews, it was similarly a no-brainer: he could not be 'the Son of God' if he died in such weakness. So why does Mark highlight the very accusations which disprove his view of Jesus (see 1:1) – which turn the inscription on the cross (v. 26) into a frightful, ironic declaration of Jesus' (and his followers') self-deception?

The heart of the answer must be that Mark believed the same as Paul – that, far from disproving Jesus' messianic status, the cross was the centrepiece of God's paradoxical wisdom, a focus of glory as well as of shame, because 'God has chosen the worthless things of the world, the despised things, the nothings and nobodies, so that he might overthrow all that seems to count' (1 Corinthians 1:28). This is the servant Son of Man 'giving his life as a ransom for many' (Mark 10:45).

But we can say more. There is huge irony in the mockery in verses 29 and 32, because we know that Jesus *will* 'come down from the cross' and gloriously rebuild the temple in three days (see John 2:20–21 – the temple of his body). Will these mockers truly see that, and believe? True faith sees the Son of God now, broken and despised on the cross. Further, Mark once again echoes the language of Psalm 22 in the way he describes and phrases the mockery: 'All who see me sneer at me… They shake their heads, "He hoped in God, let God rescue him! Let God save him, since he is on his side!"' (Psalm 22:7–8). Shaking heads is not a throwaway detail (v. 29)! The point is – precisely by their mockery, these mockers are fulfilling the prophecy which proves them wrong.

# 3 'This was the Son of God!'

**Mark 15:33–39**

The last verse of today's passage is a climax within the gospel – a counterpart to 1:11 at the start and 9:7 in the middle. But now it is not the voice of God identifying Jesus as his Son, but the unexpected voice of the centurion in charge of the executing party! And note – it's the way Jesus died that impresses this man. He sees past the shame and degradation, which for everyone else meant God's disapproval and condemnation, and sees instead something of God's own being and character displayed in Jesus.

What impressed him about the manner of Jesus' death? It's fascinating that Mark doesn't say – which means that he leaves it to his readers to work it out. What might lead us to conclude that Jesus is God's Son, as we read this account of his death?

Some suggest that the centurion saw the curtain being torn (v. 38), and it was this that impressed him. But no – Mark makes it clear that the centurion was looking at Jesus, not at the temple, and saw 'how he breathed his last' (v. 39). In any case, he could not see into the temple from Golgotha. But the tearing of the curtain might impress us, Mark's readers – especially when we notice that the voice of God in 1:11 was accompanied by another 'tearing', of the 'heavens' (1:10), so that the Holy Spirit can descend upon Jesus in baptism. And now here is Jesus, experiencing the 'baptism' of death which he foresaw (10:39), and which is marked by a second 'tearing' (the same verb) from top to bottom, another downward movement like that of the Spirit. With this symbolic division torn down, the temple can truly become 'a house of prayer for all nations' as Jesus wanted (11:17).

It's hard to know how the centurion might have been impressed by Jesus' cry of abandonment in verse 34. Like the people who think Jesus is calling for Elijah (v. 35), he wouldn't have understood the Aramaic. But we can be impressed by it: Jesus picks up the quiet fulfilments of Psalm 22 in the events surrounding his crucifixion (see 15:24, 29) and takes on to his lips the terrible cry in verse 1 of that psalm. And we might also reflect that God steps in to rescue the abandoned figure of verse 1 in response to his prayer for rescue – see Psalm 22:19–31. Verse 1 is not the end of the story…

# 4 Dead – and buried

Mark ends his gospel with another sandwich. A focus on the women who served Jesus – first by being present at his death (vv. 40–41) and then by going to anoint his body, only to find the body gone (15:47—16:8) – brackets the story of Joseph of Arimathea, who boldly acquires Jesus' body from Pilate and buries him quickly so that he does not hang on the cross through the sabbath day (vv. 42–46).

Bold service is the uniting theme here. Unlike the disciples and especially Peter, who have fled and are not present at the cross (but compare John 19:26–27), this group of women are there, despite the danger, and watching, albeit 'from a distance' (v. 40). The second Mary named here may be Jesus' mother, because he had brothers called James and Joseph, according to Mark 6:3. They have kept on 'following' (v. 41), when Jesus' male disciples have fallen away. Similarly, Joseph of Arimathea takes his life in his hands when he approaches Pilate, because all the arguments that made Peter keep quiet and deny his discipleship still apply – and even more so in Joseph's case: a Galilean fisherman could be safely ignored, but if 'a prominent member' of the Sanhedrin (v. 43) identifies himself as a follower of someone executed as an insurgent (at least officially) , he could be seized and executed to put fear into all other followers. That was the Roman style.

But this does not stop him. If he has kept his faith in Jesus quiet before, it is right out there now, publicly declared, as he approaches Pilate and asks for Jesus' body. Roman custom was to leave bodies hanging on crosses, maybe for weeks, to discourage rebellion. Joseph could have kept quiet – and then presumably the resurrection would have taken place just as his fellow Sanhedrin members had laughingly envisaged (15:32). But he acts quickly, so as to remove Jesus' body from the cross before the beginning of the Sabbath at sundown.

'Dead and buried' has been part of the Christian confession from the start (see e.g. 1 Corinthians 15:4; Romans 6:4). The 'buried' bit seems to be about finalising the death – certifying and confirming it, as the discussion in verses 44–45 shows. There was no doubt: Jesus was truly dead, so what follows was truly resurrection, not resuscitation. That hard-bitten centurion, who has already given remarkable testimony to the manner of Jesus' death (v. 39), now confirms the fact of it.

# 5 Trembling, bewildered and afraid...

We've reached the resurrection – the moment of vindication that makes sense of the suffering and completes the messianic story that Jesus has been living out: the glorious Psalm 22 rescue that God works for the abandoned one who cries out to him in faith (15:34)!

But what a strange anticlimax this passage is. We are back with the women, hurrying to the tomb and anxious about access, only to find the stone rolled back and 'a young man, dressed in a white robe, sitting on the right-hand side' of the tomb (v. 5). Their reaction is to be 'alarmed' (NIV) – surely an under-reaction! Actually the Greek is a strong word – used of Jesus in Gethsemane in 14:33 – which combines bewilderment with terror. 'Aghast' might be better. In spite of the angel's encouragement not to be 'aghast' (v. 6) and his news about the resurrection, the three women remain terrified, and Mark ends his gospel with the words, 'They came out of the tomb and fled, gripped by trembling and bewilderment. And they said nothing to anyone, for they were afraid' (v. 8) – even though the angel has given them a message for the other disciples 'and Peter' (v. 7).

What an extraordinary way to end his gospel! Tomorrow we will think about whether this was, in fact, Mark's original ending. Readers using the King James or the New King James version will note that the gospel has twelve verses yet to run (16:9–20). But there can be no doubt that these extra verses are a later addition not by Mark, as attested by all modern Bible versions, which include 16:9–20 in brackets or as a footnote. So Mark's gospel, as we have it now, ends with the words 'for they were afraid', explaining why these terrified women did *not* pass on the news of Jesus' resurrection even to the other disciples.

How amazingly encouraging this is! Of course, we know that this is not the end of the story. In Matthew, the women likewise 'leave the tomb quickly with fear', but also 'with great joy', and they run to tell the disciples – and then meet the risen Christ on the way (Matthew 28:8–9). All Mark's readers know that their fear was not the last word: but their fear was all too real! Mark thus allows us to take seriously that the message of the resurrection is indeed terrifying, because it is so completely life-changing. The good news is never easy.

# 6  Into the world!

Mark 16:9–20

We can make sense of the abrupt ending of the gospel at 16:8 (see yesterday), but it is nonetheless most odd. Can we really believe that Mark would end without a resurrection appearance of the Lord, without a 'what next?' paragraph such as we meet in all the other gospels (Matthew 28:18–20; Luke 24:44–48; John 20:30–31; 21:15–25), and on this extraordinarily negative note, the fear and silence of the first witnesses?

It is not surprising that, very early on, the oddness was felt and attempts were made to supply a proper ending. We meet a short ending – an addition to verse 8 – in just a few manuscripts of Mark ('But they gave a brief report of all these instructions to those around Peter. After that Jesus himself sent out through them, from the east as far as the west, the holy and imperishable message of eternal salvation'). The so-called 'longer ending' which we read today is found in many later manuscripts, and it became the standard text of Mark right through to the modern era, when scholars discovered that it is not included in any of the earliest and most reliable manuscripts (such as the famous Codex Sinaiticus and Codex Vaticanus) and was apparently unknown to the earliest church fathers. This, combined with its somewhat odd content and its non-Markan language (it contains 18 words that do not otherwise appear in Mark), means that it was almost certainly added to the manuscript tradition at an early date, possibly early in the second century.

But that leaves the question: is 16:8 truly Mark's original ending? It is possible that he wrote more but his manuscript was damaged, or that he intended to write more but was interrupted by the persecution under Nero and had to flee or was killed (if he was writing in Rome in the 60s, as tradition holds). Assuming he wrote more but the ending was lost, James Edwards suggests that we have a clue to his original ending in Matthew, because Matthew follows Mark very closely right up to 16:8 (= Matthew 28:8a), but then of course includes more. Edwards suggests that Matthew 28:9–10 and 16–20 contain the 'bones' of Mark's original ending (Edwards, pp. 503–504).

This ancient longer ending wants to do two things: to assure readers of the reality of the resurrection and to get the gospel launched into universal proclamation. Mark would surely have approved of this!

# Guidelines

I found these notes difficult to write, even though Mark spares us the 'gory details' of the sufferings that Jesus endured. It's very hard to follow the story through without being touched by it. What has it been like for you, reading it? The cruelty and mockery inflicted on Jesus are, of course, matched in every place where brutality is meted out to the weak, injustice is heaped on the innocent and exploitation is aimed at the poor. In what ways do you think that the message of the cross speaks particularly to today's world?

It speaks, of course, because of the amazing courage and faith of Jesus, who – despite stepping into this terrible place of abandonment where he loses everything, including all human respect and his very life – trusts God for deliverance and goes forward into the suffering with self-conscious confidence. And the resurrection is the proof that his confidence in God is not an illusion: proof that comes after, not before, the event. Are there any specific areas where you need – or could pray for others to have – that kind of confidence, courage and trust?

And as you look back over these three weeks with Mark's passion narrative – which begins with an 'anointing for burial' before Jesus dies (14:8) and ends with an attempt to anoint a corpse no longer there – what overall impression or message stays with you? How would you summarise the good news which Mark thought he was communicating (1:1)? In what ways is it good news for you, right now?

---

**FURTHER READING**

James R. Edwards, *The Gospel according to Mark* (Eerdmans/Apollos, 2002).

Paul Tillich, *The Courage To Be* (Yale University Press, 1952).

Tom Wright, *Mark for Everyone* (SPCK, 2001).

# Living in hope: Isaiah 40—55

## Walter Moberly

Some of the most memorable and moving poetry of the Old Testament can be found in Isaiah 40—55, a distinct section within the book of Isaiah as a whole. In places it has so many resonances – be it the music of Handel or images of Jesus – that its reading can be wonderfully rich.

Its context of origin appears to be the mid-sixth century BC, when the people of Judah, and its capital Jerusalem/Zion, were in exile in Babylon, after the Babylonians captured and destroyed Jerusalem in 587BC (see Jeremiah 52). In this exile, some were clearly despairing and giving up on God – 'My way is hidden from the Lord', 'The Lord has forsaken me' (40:27; 49:14). Yet, although there is stark awareness of the continuing moral and spiritual limitations of these exiles – 'I know that you are obstinate... you have never heard, you have never known' (48:4, 8) – the Lord, through the prophet, offers a future of hope and joy.

Two human agents in particular will enable this new hope. The ruler of Persia, Cyrus, will be used by the Lord to overthrow Babylon, to restore the exiles to Jerusalem and to have the temple rebuilt (44:28). And an unnamed servant of the Lord, who originally is probably the prophet himself, will renew the exiles' relationship with God, with the result that there will be servants of the Lord who will live faithfully thereafter (54:17).

The flow of the text is not always straightforward, as various unidentified voices speak, and it is not always clear how one relates to the others. For the most part, the prophet speaks in God's voice (e.g. 40:1), but sometimes he speaks in his own voice (e.g. 50:4–9), and sometimes it appears that others speak about him (e.g. 50:10; 53:1–6). Whoever speaks, the overall focus is a renewed vision of God.

Bible quotations are taken from the NRSV.

# 1  A new hope

**Isaiah 40:1–11**

God speaks. And voices cry out. Where are we? We are not told. But it may be that the prophet is in a setting such as that envisaged in Daniel 7, where the Lord is enthroned in glory and surrounded by angels who serve him. In due course, nations and their gods will be summoned here to give account (41:1, 21–24). But for now, all the focus is on what the Lord is doing for those exiles in Babylon whose home is Jerusalem.

First, God speaks reassurance, comfort for his people. The penalty for their sins is in the past, and a fresh page is now to be written. God's purposes are good (vv. 1–2).

Then an angel proclaims that mountainous desert, probably the desert to the east of Jerusalem as can be seen from the top of the Mount of Olives, is to be transformed into a smooth highway. And although no doubt this highway is to be for the exiles' home journey from Babylon, it is initially not the exiles but the Lord himself in his glory who will be seen on this road (vv. 3–5).

But when another angelic voice tells the prophet to 'cry out', the prophet is overcome by a sense of human frailty. Although the NRSV only has the prophet say, 'What shall I cry?', it is likely that the inverted commas around his words should extend to the end of verse 7 (the original text had no punctuation; translators and editors must decide). He does not know what to proclaim, because human faithfulness seems no better than weeds in the wind. Verse 8 is then the angel responding: humans are indeed frail, but in what God says there is enduring truth and reliability (vv. 6–8). The vision of reality must change.

So the prophet sounds a different note. Harking back to the picture in verses 3–5, he tells Jerusalem to climb the neighbouring Mount of Olives so that they can see, coming towards them across the desert, the Lord God who is simultaneously strong and tender (vv. 9–11).

In great poetry, images are to be taken seriously and allowed to resonate in heart and mind. As such, they can be realised in more than one way, as when the gospel writers adopt Isaiah's language to speak of preparing the way for the glory of the Lord as seen in Jesus Christ.

# 2 The incomparable God

Isaiah 40:12–31

When we pray, we can sometimes give the impression that we need to remind God of something that may have escaped his attention. So we, like the exiles, need to have our vision of God constantly refreshed. He is the one who needs no helper or advisor, the one before whom human greatness looks like emptiness (vv. 12–17). Humans too readily make idols, limited objects on which ultimate hopes are foolishly placed (vv. 18–20). Yet the God who can sweep aside human power (vv. 21–24) is also a God of attention and care, here expressed in relation to the stars, which are seemingly countless, yet each known to God (vv. 25–26).

The voice of the exiles is then heard. No incomparable God here, just one who apparently neither knows nor cares about his people (v. 27). So the prophet restates the sovereignty of Israel's God, to whose power and knowledge there are in fact no limits, however the people may feel (v. 28).

The way the prophet puts this is important. For him, theology is not something abstract, remote from everyday life and difficult to understand. Rather, what is true of God is inseparable from what can be true for humanity also. God, unlike humans, 'does not faint or grow weary'. So the first point is that the God who is strong and does not faint gives strength to people who do fail and faint – which can include even those in the prime of life, when they can feel invincible (vv. 29–30).

But what is necessary to be able to receive what God gives, so that his gift is not wasted (like sudden rain running off hard ground)? The answer is clear: it is to 'wait for' the Lord, where the Hebrew verb can also be translated 'put hope in' or 'trust in'. What is envisaged is keeping a steady and trusting focus on God, come what may. This makes all the difference, for the strength that so easily fails is thus renewed. This does not just envisage the strong action of the beating wings of an eagle. It means that people acquire the very characteristics of God himself, since they, like God, will 'not be weary' and 'not faint'. God communicates himself to the receptive, so that they can be changed and become like him. The weary and moaning can become steady and reliable. The key is to 'wait for' the Lord (v. 31).

# 3 Deliverance approaches

There are several threads that interweave throughout this chapter, which is initially presented as a trial scene (v. 1).

First, God is raising up Cyrus (not yet named) to lead Persia to victory over Babylon (vv. 2–5, 25). This will enable the exiles to return home. To recognise the pagan Cyrus as God's agent will be problematic for some, but that note will only be sounded next time Cyrus is mentioned.

Second, the idols that people make are futile (vv. 6–7, 21–24, 26–29). In the world of Babylon, the religious apparatus of temples and statues could have looked commanding to a captive people who had nothing comparable. But appearances can be misleading. Not least, the prophet appeals to God's telling 'the former things', which probably envisages the prophecies in Isaiah 1—39, where the judgement envisaged for Jerusalem's sin has now been fulfilled. No other gods have the ability to speak and act that the Lord, the God of Israel, has (vv. 21–24).

Third, there is reassurance for Israel (vv. 8–20). Although Israel may feel about as strong and significant as a worm, the Lord will give strength to his people and transform their situation.

The precise wording is significant. Israel can be confident about their future, because they ultimately depend on God's call, God's choice, of his people. In Hebrew poetry, meaning is conveyed via parallelism. A point is made, and then it is re-expressed in the next line in related wording. So here, in verse 8, 'Israel' and 'Jacob' are in parallel, as are 'my servant' and 'whom I have chosen' (and again in verse 9). What does it mean to be chosen by God? It is not for privilege but for service (though that service is a privilege).

Israel are God's chosen servant in their capacity as descendants of Abraham, whom God calls his 'friend'. Friendship means mutual delight in each other's company. Friendship with God marked Abraham, and that friendship is open also to Abraham's descendants, insofar as they follow the way of their ancestor. It is the reality that should underlie, and be expressed by, service of God. This is the point that Jesus also makes to his disciples, when he speaks of them not only as chosen and servants but also as friends (John 15:14–16). Here we are at the heart of biblical spirituality.

# 4 The vocation of God's people

Isaiah 42

Initially, the Lord speaks of Israel's vocation. God delights in, and gives his Spirit to, his people whom he has chosen (as previously, 'chosen' is parallel with, and interpreted by, 'servant'). Their task is to bring justice – the Hebrew word means 'God's right order', with a special concern for the weak and the vulnerable – to the peoples of the world. The mode of realising this vocation is also remarkable. It is not to be a matter of having the loudest or most forceful voice, but rather of being unfailingly gentle and persistent, for only so will God's right order be well established. Israel's bringing this teaching – this understanding and practice of justice – will also meet the desire and longing of nations (vv. 1–4).

Indeed, this vocation will be a light to other peoples, which will open their eyes and set them free from their bondage to false realities. Then at last they will become able to see the one true sovereign God, the Lord (vv. 5–9). The vision of this reality leads the prophet to call for song, in joyful celebration of something so wonderful (vv. 10–12).

But how is this new reality to come about? How can the despondent exiles in Babylon even begin to conceive of themselves in such a role? First and foremost, it depends upon God. God will act like a mighty warrior (maybe in line with the vision of Psalm 46:8–10, where the divine power destroys conventional weapons of war). God will transform the situation and lead his people in new ways. Then they will see afresh that alternatives to God are worthless (vv. 13–17).

All this is said, however, with full realisation that Israel is far from being a people who are faithfully responsive to God. On the contrary, their hearts and minds are dull and hard: they see without seeing and hear without hearing (vv. 18–20). Indeed, because of waywardness and disobedience, the Lord gave his people into the power of Babylon. Yet even the shock and pain of this made no real difference: 'It burned him, but he did not take it to heart' (vv. 21–25).

There is thus a deep tension between God's vision of his people and their vocation, and the disappointing moral and spiritual limitations that consti-tute their present reality. How to make progress beyond this impasse is a key concern in the coming chapters.

# 5 Delight and disappointment

'But now…' The prophet starts with a sharp contrast to the low note on which the previous chapter ended. Memorable images of God's care for, and joy in, his people flow from the prophet's lips. Powerful natural forces that would normally destroy them will not do so. God would gladly trade other wealthy and exotic nations for this one people in whom he specially delights. Wherever they have been scattered since the overthrow of Jerusalem (even if many are currently in Babylon), God will gather his people together. Astonishingly, God has made this people 'for my glory' – so that his name will be honoured on account of this particular people. Some realisation of the prayer 'Hallowed be thy name' can come through the life and witness of God's people (vv. 1–7).

A renewed vision of God remains the first thing that Israel needs. They must see afresh for themselves that the Lord is the one true God, the only one in whom life and truth can be found. When they have seen this for themselves, they can then be witnesses to others, so that they too can come to know this. He alone is the God of sovereign power (vv. 8–13).

Specific reassurance is given in terms of the coming overthrow of Babylon. This will then lead to a kind of renewal of the ancient exodus from Egypt, only this time it will be better – not just springs of water but whole rivers in the desert, so that God's people will not be lacking. Rather, they will celebrate the greatness of their Lord (vv. 14–21).

And yet… As previously, these images of a joyful future are juxtaposed with a reminder of the disappointment that Israel currently is. The people who should witness to God and declare his praise have burdened him with their sins and even, as it were, wearied the one who does not grow weary (40:28) with their constant failures in faithfulness (vv. 22–24).

God summons Israel to present their case against him. If they can, let them show that he in any way fails in his faithfulness – either in his merciful forgiveness or in his acts of judgement that call Israel to account (vv. 25–28).

Again, we are left with an unresolved tension between two different visions of reality. For us, as for the ancient recipients of the prophet's message, this is a call to shake off complacency.

# 6 The nature of monotheism

Whatever the persistence of Israel in their spiritual blindness, the persistence of God in his grace is greater. So this chapter begins with another 'But now…' to underline God's resolution to move beyond his people's failures. Reassurance is given, despite their continuing fears. There is another illuminating poetic parallelism in verse 3, where 'spirit' is paralleled with 'blessing': the Lord's presence is for the good of his people, to enhance their living and enable their flourishing. The result will be people's grateful willingness to be identified as the particular people of God (vv. 1-5).

As previously, a vision of Israel's flourishing is accompanied by a renewed vision of God as the one and only (vv. 6-8). We can easily think of belief in only one God ('monotheism') as something rather abstract, with a theoretical denial of the existence of other gods. Yet the prophet's emphasis that there is no other god is akin to a speaker saying to an audience, 'We have no choice,' or, 'There is no other way.' Theoretically there is always a choice, always another way. Yet the concern is to urge the acceptance of one way as better than any other. The prophet's concern is practical, that Israel look to the Lord alone, as the only one who speaks to and strengthens them. Other parts of the Old Testament regularly warn of the danger of other gods, who are not simply non-existent. There are always identities other than 'I am the Lord's', and people or things other than the Lord on whom hearts and minds can be set.

In this prophet's context the challenge was the impressive-looking religious apparatus of Babylon, which might seduce Israel's imagination. So there is an extended passage on the folly of idols and idol making. The point is not to attempt a sympathetic understanding of what Babylonians were doing in their religious practices. It is rather a deterrent, a dissuasion, to Israel, a way of saying, 'Don't go there!', which is better served by a degree of mockery than by thoughtful analysis. If Israel is soon to be leaving Babylon, it must start detaching itself (vv. 9-20).

So the section ends with a renewed call to Israel to focus on their God, the only one who saves them. And this leads into a note of song, in joyful wonder at what the Lord does for his people (vv. 21-23).

# Guidelines

We have seen a repeated contrast in these chapters. On the one hand, there is the Lord's vision of his people, the chosen object of his delight, his servants to make his ways known in the world; and there is the prophet's vision of the Lord, the incomparable sovereign God, who speaks and acts faithfully and who is going to deliver his people. On the other hand, there is the dismal reality of a people of small moral and spiritual stature, more inclined to moan about a God who seems unconcerned than to see him truly or to serve him. For many of us, this will ring some bells with what we see of the life of the churches around us in contrast to what we see in scripture or in a few contexts of flourishing. The gap between what we are and what we should be is painful – and rightly so, for otherwise we will never do anything about it.

One specific thing that the prophet says can be done is to 'wait for the Lord' (40:31), which we noted to have the sense of hope and trust, both patient and lively. This enables people to acquire something of the character of the Lord himself, in terms of faithful endurance. This is a recurrent keynote in the Psalms, which repeatedly encourage waiting for the Lord (and there are many strong resonances and linkages between the book of Isaiah and the Psalms). A fine example is Psalm 130, where, before telling Israel to 'hope in the Lord', the psalmist says of himself: 'I wait for the Lord, my soul waits, and in his word I hope; my soul waits for the Lord more than those who watch for the morning, more than those who watch for the morning' (vv. 5–6). Those who have to stay awake through the night on guard duty *really* want the morning to come.

Can we be like the psalmist, as a way of entering into what the prophet says? Can we resolve to 'wait for the Lord' – being patient in prayer, hopeful in outlook, trusting amid difficulties, in confidence that if we do so we will enter more fully into God's good purposes for us and for others?

# 1 God's surprising ways

Isaiah 44:24—45:8

A new development now emerges, a next step in God's message to Jerusalem and the exiles in Babylon. Previously, we heard of God's raising up a victorious figure who will sweep all before him (41:2–5, 25). This now becomes specific: the victorious figure is Cyrus, known to history as the ruler of Persia and conqueror of Babylon in the sixth century BC. God's purpose in using him is the restoration and rebuilding of Jerusalem and the towns of Judah. In other words, Cyrus will encourage the captives to return home and renew their life around the temple in Jerusalem, and this will fulfil the Lord's promises to his people (44:24–28).

After speaking to Israel *about* Cyrus, the prophet then, as it were, speaks *to* Cyrus. We have no way of knowing whether Cyrus ever was aware of this message from an Israelite prophet. Probably the significant thing is that this address enables the prophet to say more about the Lord's purposes with Cyrus (45:1–7).

Four points are noteworthy. First, Cyrus is called God's 'anointed', a term usually used of David and his descendants as kings of Jerusalem – and a term that will eventually depict the role of God's appointed saviour, 'the Messiah' (which in Hebrew means 'anointed one', as does 'Christ' in Greek). Second, God can use Cyrus, whether or not Cyrus recognises the fact or acknowledges the God who is directing him ('I arm you, though you do not know me'). Thus an explicitly pagan ruler is God's chosen agent to deliver Israel from Babylon. Third, what God is doing through Cyrus is to bring widespread recognition of the Lord as the one true God. Fourth, the prophet reiterates God's sovereign power to use Cyrus (45:7). The wording here has a long history of controversy, as it has often been taken to be making the problematic claim that God creates 'evil'. Yet the point of the second line of verse 7 is that God brings both good times ('peace') and hard times ('woe'), times when kingdoms flourish and times when they are overthrown: God is the Lord of history.

Finally, there is a joyous exclamation to celebrate the good things that the Lord is bringing to his people in exile (45:8).

# 2 Objection overruled

Some of the prophet's contemporaries were apparently not happy with his message. They want to challenge what they hear God saying through him. What was the problem? It was almost certainly God's use of Cyrus and designation of him as 'anointed', a term usually reserved for the Davidic kings of Jerusalem. This clearly felt wrong, perhaps blasphemous ('How could you possibly say that of an ignorant pagan?'). Yet the prophet responds by reiterating both that God has sovereign power and that Cyrus is indeed the one who will set the exiles free and rebuild Jerusalem. Moreover, this deliverance through Cyrus will cost the exiles precisely nothing (vv. 9–13).

Not only will the exiles be released, but also roles will be reversed. Instead of being captives, Israel will have other nations bowing down to them and acknowledging that their God is the one true God (v. 14). The next verse (v. 15) has often been used as a free-standing axiom about God as a hidden God. Its precise force in context is in fact hard to gauge, and part of the problem is that it is unclear who is speaking, the nations of the previous verse or the prophet himself. Perhaps its force in context is to underline that God's saving ways can be surprising, not least in that what happens on the ground is often more mundane than some of the prophet's glowing poetic images.

In any case, the prophet continues with an affirmation of God's saving power over against the futility of idols, and a further affirmation of the reliability of what the Lord says (vv. 16–19). This leads to a climactic summons to the peoples of the earth generally to recognise the Lord, the God of Israel, as the one true God, the only one in whom justice and salvation are found (vv. 20–25). This is expressed as strongly as possible in terms of an unshakeable divine oath – that peoples around the world will reverently acknowledge the Lord (v. 23). Precisely what the prophet envisaged in his sixth-century context is unclear; perhaps he sees it as related to his own ministry. But in the New Testament Paul is in no doubt that it is the crucified and risen Jesus who is to be the focal point of this recognition of ultimate truth and life in the one God (Philippians 2:9–11).

# 3 Who carries whom?

As noted last week, the splendour of Babylon – its buildings, its wealth, its ceremonies – could easily have overpowered the imagination of the exiled Israelites: 'Maybe this is where real power and hope for the future is to be found.' So the prophet continues to renew their vision of the Lord, the one true God.

His initial move here is to use satire, to mock what can look so impressive. The images of the Babylonian gods, seemingly so magnificent, are no more than burdens for struggling animals to carry. By contrast, the Lord is not carried but carries; he is the one who carries Israel from their first moments to their last. He is the one who is utterly dependable, who will not fail those he has made his people (vv. 1–4).

The prophet further develops the satirical contrast by inviting the Israelites to imagine the seemingly impressive processes involved in constructing the images of the Babylonian deities: expensive materials, professional craftsmen, a process culminating in ceremony and spectacle. But there is a fundamental problem: the image is dumb and impotent. So people's prayers and needs are ignored and uncared for (vv. 5–7).

By contrast, the Lord is the incomparable God. To turn anywhere other than to him is ultimately futile. He is the one with an overriding purpose for his people, a purpose that started before this generation and that will continue beyond it. It is a purpose that entails deliverance and salvation, to be brought about in the immediate context through Cyrus. No matter how slow and resistant Israel may be ('transgressors', 'stubborn of heart'), the Lord will realise his good purposes for them (vv. 8–13).

The idols of ancient religion are not an issue in the contemporary world. But the fundamental meaning of idolatry is to treat as God what is not God, to set one's heart on something in creation – a person, idea, sport, movement, pleasure or whatever – as though it could enable fullness of life in the way that only the creator God can. Believers today can easily be awed and imaginatively overwhelmed by the achievements of technological society (which of course have real value when used rightly) and so lose sight of the true God as the one to receive our deepest hope and trust for both time and eternity.

# 4 The overthrow of Babylon

After mocking the gods of Babylon, their supposed ultimate security, the prophet now spells out what is in store for the city of Babylon and its inhabitants. It will be an overturning of what they are accustomed to – as when a wealthy woman, accustomed to luxury and being waited on, becomes a menial servant who has to do the hardest and most unwelcome chores. Although Cyrus will be the human agent of this, it is the Lord who will be at work through him (vv. 1–4).

Why will such a terrible fate come on Babylon? The prophet gives two prime reasons: cruelty and complacent arrogance.

First, it is how the Babylonians used their power when they had it. Their attitude to captive Israel is summarised succinctly: 'You showed them no mercy.' Indeed, those who were especially vulnerable, the aged who no longer had the strength to do what they would want, were particularly victimised. Power exercised self-servingly, without care for others, corrupts and corrodes life. And the Babylonians acted thus in a complacent assurance that their power was not itself finite and transient (vv. 5–7).

Second, their complacency is depicted more fully in terms of Babylon supposing itself to have the kind of ultimate power and security that only God has. Twice Babylon is depicted as saying, 'I am, and there is no one besides me.' This is the language that the Lord uses of himself, the truth of which he wants Israel to recognise (43:11; 44:8; 45:22). As with the Lord's words, which are not a theoretical denial of the existence of other gods, Babylon's words are not a denial of the existence of nations other than Babylon. Rather, they are a claim that none of them matter in comparison, for Babylon's greatness is beyond challenge. Nonetheless, an overthrow of which they cannot conceive will indeed come upon them (vv. 8–11).

The prophet rounds off with heavy irony, telling the Babylonians to persist with their familiar ways, for all the good it will do them. He has already made clear that there is an alternative (45:22), but presumably the Babylonians are not yet ready to hear it (vv. 12–15).

In today's world certain powers – whether political and military, or economic and technological – may seem beyond challenge. Yet if we learn from this prophet, we will see that such things are not really as they appear to be.

# 5  The problem that doesn't easily go away

Isaiah 48:1–16

In the last few chapters the prophet has offered glowing images of God's good purposes for his exiled people. Cyrus will come and overthrow Babylon; Babylonian power and confidence will be overturned; Babylonian gods are not worth worrying about; and the Lord is doing something that can lead to other nations recognising the reality and reliability of Israel's God.

Yet a basic problem remains: the people of Israel themselves. They are indeed the people of the Lord, and look to him. But they do so 'not in truth or right'. This sounds a keynote which the next few verses develop (vv. 1–2).

God's purposes have long since been declared by his prophets, perhaps especially the content recorded in the first half of the book of Isaiah (which may be the prime referent of 'the former things'). Those words, especially the warning of judgement for faithlessness, have been realised. Similar things are again happening as the prophet now speaks to them. Yet instead of Israel learning from all this, they have remained unresponsive, even treacherous (vv. 3–8).

So what is the Lord to do with such an unpromising people? First and foremost, he does not give up. He does not angrily throw Israel aside, but rather tests and refines them, so that eventually they will indeed learn and become able to respond truly to their God with astonished praise (vv. 9–11).

The prophet then summarises what he has said so far about the unique sovereignty of the one God, the God who is Lord of all, and who is currently raising up Cyrus to deliver Israel from Babylon in line with his good purposes for them (vv. 12–16a).

What is to be done about this apparent impasse between the Lord's purposes and Israel's sheer unresponsiveness? In the last line of this section a new note is sounded. Previously the 'I' has always been the Lord (through the prophet). Now, for the first time, there is a different 'I' who speaks in his own name, and speaks of being empowered to speak and act on God's behalf: 'And now the Lord God has sent me and his spirit' (v. 16b). This is best understood as the voice of the prophet himself, in his own right. He has been called and commissioned to do something to resolve the impasse.

# 6  A first glimpse of the prophet-servant's vocation

**Isaiah 48:17—49:13**

Initially, there is a general reminder of things that Israel should know. God's purposes for Israel are good; listening to and learning from their God would bring Israel's flourishing; and God's leading of Israel in the exodus from Egypt provides the pattern of what he can and will do again (48:17–21).

An isolated note of warning is then sounded: 'There is no peace… for the wicked' (48:22). A similar note is sounded later (57:21). The first note comes about a third of the way through Isaiah 40—66, and the second note about two-thirds of the way. Perhaps the two verses were added as part of the structuring of Isaiah 40—66 as a whole. But however that may be, the content is a warning to the heedless and corrupt.

Now the voice that first spoke in its own right in 48:16b speaks further. He tells of a special vocation from the Lord, a vocation of significance not just for Israel for the world generally (49:1–7).

If his call is from before birth, it means that his whole life is purposed by God for this vocation, which is no mere passing stage of life (49:1, 5). Indeed, the vocation of Israel as the people of God, called to serve and glorify God and be a light to others (42:6), has devolved specifically upon him (49:3). Yet the call is paradoxical – although he has been given ability to speak words that cut to the heart, he has also been hidden away (49:2). This has led to his feeling that all he has done has been worthless – until he reassures himself of the Lord's faithfulness (49:4). His first task is to overcome the impasse of Israel's unresponsiveness, and to restore Israel to be what they should be. Yet he is called to do even more, and be the channel of God's light and salvation for all peoples (49:5–6). In this way he can realise the Lord's earlier summons to the ends of the earth (45:22). The Lord then reassures the prophet-servant that, even if his vocation entails being despised, he will ultimately gain a life-changing response even from the mighty, because of the Lord's faithfulness to his call (49:7).

In the first instance, however, this prophet-servant is to enable the return of Israel from exile as a first step in their deeper restoration (49:8–13).

# Guidelines

One of the challenges in interpreting Isaiah 40—55 is to know how best to understand its sweeping poetic imagery.

On the one hand, there is the issue of seeing how poetry appeals to the imagination in ways that can differ from prose. In general terms, this involves taking language seriously without taking it woodenly (or 'literally', which is a word that tends to create more problems than it solves in biblical interpretation). If the mind takes an image seriously, and allows it to linger imaginatively, it can make a difference to how we see things in life generally. Images become ways of making sense of the often complex and messy realities of everyday life. For many people today, strong images come less from poetry as such than from novels and TV and films: Harry Potter, Hogwarts and Voldemort; Jedi knights and the Force; James Bond and espionage, etc. These have their place. But a challenge for Christians is to allow scripture to function thus, so that it is not primarily a repository of predictable dos and don'ts, but rather an imaginative world that we inhabit and use to make sense of our everyday world in the light of God and God's priorities.

On the other hand, there is the question of how prophetic poetry relates to the known realities of history and life. We know something of what happened when the exiles returned to Jerusalem from Babylon through books like Ezra and Nehemiah, Haggai and Zechariah. What happened on the ground is much more limited, disappointing even, than one might have expected from sweeping images of the desert being transformed and other peoples acknowledging Israel and its God. Yet the prophetic poetry is surely meant less as a predictive description of imminent events (though there is of course an element of that) than as the formation of a spiritual and moral vision of God and his good purposes. It offers a vision of ultimate realities and priorities, in which hope can be placed and in the light of which one can live now. Such a vision can be affirmed even when what is happening on the ground may be bitty and disappointing.

Amid all the glorious pictures that scripture offers, we, like the prophet-servant, live by faith not sight.

# 1 The faithfulness of the Lord and of his servant

**Isaiah 49:14—50:11**

Today's reading falls into two distinct sections. First, there is the Lord's reassurance to the people of Zion/Jerusalem, who are still inclined to doubt his good purposes for them (49:14—50:3). Second, there is further personal testimony from the prophet himself in his role as the faithful servant who will enable the realisation of God's will for both Israel and the world (50:4–11).

Zion's continuing despair (49:14), a note sounded at the outset (40:27), is met with unconditional reassurance. The Lord has, as it were, a picture of the walls and buildings of Jerusalem inscribed on his hands, so that he sees it constantly and will thus enable the restoration of the ruined city (49:14–21). Like so much else, this has strong resonances with the New Testament, when we think of the nail-marks still on the hands of the risen Christ, as the indelible sign of his care for us.

Indeed, the Lord's restoration of Zion will involve overcoming its enemies, who will acknowledge Zion's renewal. The Lord has absolutely not abandoned his people, and by his transformative power, as in the exodus, he will restore them (49:22—50:3).

Yet the picture of divine power now transitions to the testimony of the servant, where things initially look very different. He has learned to speak words of life to others through the daily discipline each morning of listening to God, somewhat like the Israelites in the desert collecting manna afresh every morning (50:4; Exodus 16). Yet the immediate response to his words of life is not gratitude or joy but scornful and brutal opposition (50:5–6). The servant's faithfulness has a high cost. He does not lose heart, however, because his trust in God and God's sustenance matters more than everything else (50:7–9).

This then leads to a searching question: who will heed this servant who utterly trusts God even in the midst of unrelieved darkness? He, and those who heed him, have a sure future which those who scornfully oppose him will not have (50:10–11). This question is asked by a different voice in the text. It appears to be the voice of those who themselves have heeded, who have become servants of the Lord (54:17b) with a faith in God renewed by the person and work of the faithful prophet-servant.

# 2 Lamentation turns to joy

This chapter revolves around commands. Initially (vv. 1–8), there are repeated commands to listen (vv. 1, 4, 7) and look (vv. 2, 6). Although previously Israel has failed to hear and see (42:18–20; 48:8), something different is now happening. In particular, those who are summoned to listen are those who 'know righteousness' and have God's teaching in their hearts (v. 7). This suggests that the prophet-servant may be specifically addressing those other servants who are already responding to him and finding through him renewed faith and life (their voice was heard in 50:10). This would mean that the assurances to Zion, although still intended for Zion as a whole, are now focused specifically on those who are already learning, through the prophet-servant, to be what the people of Zion should be, just as the prophet-servant himself was called to embody the vocation of Israel as a whole (49:3). They are to have a clear vision of God's enduring and unfailing good purposes (vv. 6, 8). The precedent of God's blessing of Abraham, given at such a time when he had nothing and no one other than Sarah, remains valid for God's people now (vv. 2–3).

The prophet then boldly commands God with a repeated imperative! (Such is the liberty of one who is faithful in extremity and also a poet; John Donne did similarly.) He summons the Lord to show his strength and renew the power he showed in the exodus by restoring the exiles to Zion – a deliverance which will bring deep and lasting joy (vv. 9–11).

The Lord then responds to this with the same note of comfort that opens this whole section of the book of Isaiah, and he reiterates the theme of his sovereign power (vv. 12–15). He also briefly addresses the prophet-servant, to link his vocation with both the overall greatness of creation and the specific restoration of Zion (v. 16).

The next imperative (also repeated) is to Zion/Jerusalem: those who have staggered and fallen must rise and stand in a way that for long has not been possible (vv. 17–23). The depiction of Jerusalem here has many resonances with the depiction of Jerusalem in the book of Lamentations. It is likely that the prophet specifically has the content of that book in mind, and thereby emphasises that that awfulness of Jerusalem's condition in the aftermath of Babylonian victory is definitively at an end.

# 3 The deliverance of Jerusalem is now

In a sense, this section is the climax of what the prophet, on God's behalf, has been saying since chapter 40. The time for the restoration of Jerusalem, and the restoration of the exiles from Babylon, has come.

It starts with another repeated imperative, again addressed to Zion. She is to arise and be beautiful. This new beauty is to be accompanied by a new purity, a freedom from what had been defiling her. The fallen one is to rise and stand in freedom (vv. 1–2). It is a picture of the Lord's delight in his people.

There is then a paragraph, in prose, unlike the surrounding poetry, which is slightly surprising in its role here (vv. 3–6). It focuses on the notion of gratuity. The ease with which Jerusalem had been conquered by the Babylonians is depicted as being 'sold for nothing' and 'without cause' (vv. 3, 5; the same Hebrew word is used each time). So also what the Lord will do will be nothing like any kind of economic transaction, such as buying back a slave. Rather, it will be the kind of action that enables a fresh recognition of a gracious God (vv. 3, 6).

We then return to the famous images of chapter 40, excitedly reprised here: the loveliness of the messenger with his message of God's sovereign rule; joyful singing as people see the Lord himself returning to his city; the restoration of that city; and a vision of God's majesty and power that extends beyond Israel to the world as a whole (vv. 7–10). It is reprised here because now it is to be realised.

For the final repeated imperatives envisage the people of Jerusalem no longer preparing to depart but actually departing: 'go out'. The time has come. This is not a moment of fluster lest it be missed, but a progression ordered and protected by God, whose deliverance is sure (vv. 11–12).

Specific mention is made of 'carrying the vessels of the Lord', those implements that enabled Israel's worship in the temple. To many a modern mind, they might sound unimportant. Yet Ezra 1:7–11 and 5:14–15 provide an impressive inventory, and portray Cyrus himself recognising their importance. They symbolise both the continuity of former patterns of worship in a new context and the value of beauty in worship.

# 4  The suffering servant

Isaiah 52:13—53:12

The climax of the exiles' departure from Babylon still leaves unfinished the account of the unique role of the prophet as servant of the Lord and his enduring impact.

Initially, we are told that the prophet-servant will be exalted in a way analogous to the Lord in the temple (6:1) and that he will have a huge impact on many peoples, even if initially they saw in him nothing attractive (52:13–15).

The astonishing ministry of the servant is depicted by others ('we'), presumably again those who have themselves become servants through his ministry. The initial note they sound is one of astonishment. How could someone whose unattractive appearance and physical infirmity were a turn-off possibly be a decisive channel for the Lord's power? Everyone's initial inclination, including that of those now speaking, was to write him off (53:1–3).

Yet this leads into an astonished recognition. Those who are now servants had initially reckoned that if the prophet-servant suffered, it must have been because he had done something wrong for which God afflicted him. But they have come to see that it was *their* wrongdoing, not that of the prophet himself, that was the cause of his suffering. Somehow, the terrible things he went through was the outworking of *their* actions – and yet *they* are the ones who now have healing and life (53:4–6).

What this meant for the prophet-servant is depicted with images that suggest a trial which was a massive miscarriage of justice. Groundless accusations, which he endured silently, resulted in a death penalty and the subsequent execution of an innocent man (53:7–9).

Yet somehow this death was not the end, but a way to a new and unprecedented realisation of God's good purposes: 'Through him the will of the Lord shall prosper.' Indeed, this man who knew what it was to live rightly with God has enabled others also to become what he was: 'The righteous one, my servant, shall make many righteous.' They have recognised that his self-giving to death was for the lasting benefit of others who did not deserve what they have received from him (53:10–12).

Much is left to the imagination in this remarkable testimony. But it is hardly surprising that Christians down the centuries have seen in this prophet-servant the clear outline of Jesus.

# 5 The servant's faithfulness gives rise to other servants

We return to the restoration of Zion, who is the female figure addressed throughout, in the light of what has been said about the accomplishment of the prophet-servant. Nothing further is said about Zion's past failings or desolation. The images are all of her flourishing, security and peace.

First, those who inhabit Zion will become numerous. Indeed, they will become so many that the city will have to be enlarged to contain them all, and they will also spill over and possess other territories also, in a way reminiscent of God's promises to faithful Abraham (vv. 1–3; compare Genesis 22:17).

Second, the Lord's relationship with his people, like that of husband and wife after a difficult period, will be renewed. Although the exile felt like bereavement and widowhood, and the Lord indeed had been angry with his people, God's faithfulness is being renewed enduringly, so that the recent traumas will seem but a short passing episode (vv. 4–8).

Third, there is the precedent of God's commitment in the context of Noah. God's promise that never again would the earth be flooded (Genesis 9:8–17) is analogous to his reassurance now. Even if those solid and enduring elements of the world, mountains and hills, should cease to be solid and somehow crumble or move, the Lord's compassion will never crumble or go away (vv. 9–10). A future more stable than mountains awaits.

Fourth, Zion's future is depicted with images of wealth, beauty and security from enemies (vv. 11–17a). Strikingly, Zion's children, her future inhabitants, will be 'taught by the Lord' (v. 13), which is exactly what characterised the prophet-servant in his testimony about what enabled him to realise his vocation (50:4). There is thus a clear sense that that quality of walking with God that marked the servant will mark others too in future.

So it is not surprising that the final note of the chapter is to affirm that all these promises to Zion are 'the heritage of the servants of the Lord' (v. 17b). We earlier noted (Day 2) that these servants embody and represent Zion in the way that the prophet-servant was called to embody and represent Israel (49:3). These plural servants appear to be the fruit of the life and work of the singular prophet-servant, those who have entered into the new reality he has brought about under God.

# 6 Seize the moment

The dominant emphases in Isaiah 40—55 have been on what the Lord is doing for his people and the role of the prophet-servant in this. Yet it is vital that people respond to God's initiative. Complacency, heedlessness or just wallowing in a feeling of hopelessness make for moral and spiritual death. We have already seen repeated imperatives in chapters 51 and 52 ('listen', 'rouse yourself', 'awake', 'go out'). Imperatives and the need to respond are the keynote also of this final chapter, even as the Lord's promises and reassurances are also reiterated.

The initial imperative is to eat and drink. Food and drink are fundamental necessities for life to be sustained, and so are ready metaphors for what matters most. It is all too easy to misdirect one's quest for life's basics and not realise that the deepest satisfaction is never something to be bought but only a gift of grace (vv. 1–2).

The next imperative is to hear and respond to a renewed promise of what God is doing for his people. As he enabled David to be widely recognised as a great leader, so he will make Israel a widely respected people, so that their glory reflects God's own glory (vv. 3–5). True response to God involves trust in his promises.

The third and final imperative is to seize the moment: 'Seek the Lord while he may be found, call upon him while he is near.' In the abstract, there is an obvious puzzle here: is not God always present everywhere? Yet we know that in regular life – in work, politics, romance, family relationships, personal struggles – there come key moments when what we decide and do shapes what happens subsequently. So too with God; if a moment of openness and opportunity is not taken, it can pass and we can be left stuck in our own mud. We will never fully grasp how and why things are thus, because God's ways are beyond our comprehension. But that is no excuse for not acting upon what we do know (vv. 6–9).

The prophet then summarises his message. The divine word that he has proclaimed is not only enduring (40:8) but also fruitful and life-giving. This is the reality given to Israel. And so the restoration of the exiles, who thought they had lost everything, will be a moment of wondrous joy (vv. 10–13).

# Guidelines

On the road to Emmaus, Jesus famously spoke to his two uncomprehending disciples about 'the things about himself in all the scriptures' (Luke 24:27). We are not told which passages he interpreted or how he did so. For Christians down the ages, the Isaianic depictions of the suffering yet faithful servant of the Lord have usually been at the top of the list. It is not hard to see why, as the resonances between the Isaianic servant and Jesus in his passion are so obvious and strong.

The nature of the relationship between the servant and Jesus has been much discussed. Although sometimes Christians have supposed that the Old Testament is here predicting Jesus, what is said about the faithful servant is not depicted as in the future (like the exiles leaving Babylon) except in terms of impact (52:13–15; 53:10–12). The servant speaks in his own voice about what he has gone through, and others speak in terms of what they have already learned from him. Indeed, I have suggested that the text makes best sense if it is the prophet himself who is seen as the servant and that it is his disciples who commend him as the one in whom they have encountered and come to understand God's surprising ways that initially made no sense to them. Thus the portrayal of the servant is not a prediction but a pattern, a supreme model of what right response to God looks like. Jesus, whose faithful responsiveness to his Father is unbroken ('without sin', Hebrews 4:15), supremely embodies and realises that of which Isaiah speaks.

But if Jesus is the supreme embodiment, he is not the only embodiment. The call to enter into what scripture speaks of remains for all. We too are called to become faithful servants of the Lord. Although this brings joy, it can also bring hardship, possibly at levels undreamt of. To 'walk in darkness' and have 'no light', yet trust 'in the name of the Lord' and rely upon God (Isaiah 50:10) reminds us that the heart of truth about God and our life with God is seen in Gethsemane and Calvary.

---

**FURTHER READING**

Walter Brueggemann, *Isaiah*, Vol. 2 (Westminster John Knox Press, 1998).

John Goldingay, *The Message of Isaiah 40—55: A literary-theological commentary* (T&T Clark, 2005).

Christopher Seitz, 'The Book of Isaiah 40–66' in Leander Keck et al. (eds), *The New Interpreter's Bible*, Vol. 6 (Abingdon Press, 2001).

Claus Westermann, *Isaiah 40—66* (SCM, 1969).

# Vulnerable children in the Old Testament

Tim Davy

The Bible has much to say about the experiences of children and young people who are living at the margins of society. As we will see in this short series of studies focusing on Old Testament texts, the plight of vulnerable children is close to the heart of God and, therefore, working with and on behalf of such young people is a core commitment he expects to be present in the life of his people.

While all of us will have a degree of vulnerability in our lives, by 'vulnerable children' or 'children-at-risk' I am referring to children and young people who, in the words of the Lausanne Movement's Children-at-Risk forum, 'experience an intense and/or chronic risk factor, or a combination of risk factors in personal, environmental and/or relational domains that prevent them from pursuing and fulfilling their God-given potential' (**lausanne.org/content/statement/children-at-risk-missional-definition**).

Being attentive to the plight and needs of young people like these is important, whether they are to be found in the pages of the Bible or on the fringes of our own societies. In both cases they are often overlooked.

This brief series will touch on a variety of texts, including law, narrative, prophetic oracle and song. Many other texts could have been chosen, but the selection should give you an entry point into the material. Perhaps by paying closer attention to their stories in the biblical texts, this will attune us to their stories in our neighbourhoods as well.

Some of the material from these studies appeared previously in a Redcliffe College Bible study resource, 'More than a Statistic: God's heart for displaced and vulnerable children'. Used with permission.

Bible quotations are taken from the ESV.

# 1 Moses and Miriam

**Exodus 1:15—2:10**

Our first story of child vulnerability demonstrates only too well how the lives of children and young people are usually caught up in the machinations of those much more powerful than they.

At the beginning of the Exodus story, we find out that the people of Israel have now been in Egypt for many years and have multiplied greatly, but their initial welcome has given way to bitter enslavement. The unnamed king of Egypt, fearful of the strength of the Israelites, commands a brutal policy to control the population. He decrees that midwives should become executioners, but the two named Hebrew midwives (Shiphrah and Puah) claim they never arrive in time. Pharaoh then charges 'all his people' to throw every male born to the Hebrews into the Nile (1:22).

As we might have done while reading through Genesis, with all the ups and downs of the family dynamics of the patriarchs, we could ask here at the start of the book of Exodus, 'Is there a future for the people of God?' Yet it was into the horrific context of state-sponsored infanticide that Moses, Israel's future leader, was born.

Throughout our passage, Pharaoh's plans to exterminate all male babies are thwarted by the ingenuity, bravery and compassion of female characters: the midwives, Moses' mother, Moses' sister Miriam and finally (and ironically) Pharaoh's own daughter. Given our focus on vulnerable children, we will concentrate our attention on Miriam.

It isn't clear what his mother expected by placing Moses in a basket on the water. Did she know that there was a chance of Pharaoh's daughter finding him and having compassion on him? Was Miriam instructed to station herself and watch for Pharaoh's daughter, or was this all the young girl's idea? Whatever the case, Miriam takes the bold – audacious, even – step and seizes her opportunity. Pharaoh's daughter moves from curiosity to pity. But it is Miriam's question in 2:7 that seems to move her from pity to action, thereby saving and securing a future for her brother.

Would an adult have got away with making the kind of suggestion Miriam offers? It could be that Miriam, herself vulnerable to some degree, plays a role here that only a child could play.

# 2 What does the Lord require?

Deuteronomy 10:12–22

In today's study we move from narrative to a sermon that gets to the heart of God's core commitment to vulnerable children.

We join the people of Israel on the edge of the promised land. In Deuteronomy, Moses preaches to the people, urging them to shape their new society in the land in a way that pleases God and demonstrates his ways to the watching world (see, for example, Deuteronomy 4).

Just before setting out a whole range of laws to achieve this, Moses lays out a challenge to the people. It has a neat structure, with two 'bookends' in verses 12–13 and 20–22 that charge the people of Israel to maintain a committed, loving and faithful pursuit of God's requirements and to trust in his own faithfulness to them.

The central section has a a triplet of verse pairings: an outline of something significant about God's rule (vv. 14, 17); a reflection on the beneficiaries of that rule (vv. 15, 18); and the reasonable response of Israel (vv. 16, 19).

Verses 17–19 are our focus. Who is highlighted as benefiting from the incalculable might and authority of God (v. 17)? Not the royal elite, but the fatherless, the widow and the alien (v. 18). This grouping reflected the most vulnerable in that society. They all had one thing in common: the lack or loss of a living adult male, who was essential at that time for ensuring their protection, provision and inclusion. Regardless of how they arrived at those circumstances, they relied on the hospitality and commitment of others to protect and provide for them.

The call to show love and justice towards the marginalised is here depicted as a response both to God's own character and also to Israel's own 'outsider' experience in Egypt. Caring for the marginalised and vulnerable is a reflection of who God is and what he is committed to. If that was not sufficient motivation for Israel, their memory should also fuel their compassion and solidarity. They knew as a people what it was like to receive hospitality, and they knew what it was like to be subject to hostility. Now that they were about to be given a land of their own and were about to become potential hosts, they must carry out their God-reflecting responsibilities towards the outsider and the vulnerable.

# 3  Debt and deliverance

In the following pair of studies we will use stories from the book of 2 Kings that depict different sets of circumstances in which children in ancient Israel were particularly vulnerable: economic debt and warfare. Both stories have a miraculous element and occur during the prophetic ministry of Elisha.

In 2 Kings 4 we read about the widow of one of the 'sons of the prophets' (see 2 Kings 2), who has fallen into debt. In the ancient world, there were not many options available to you if you were unable to repay your creditors, so selling your children and, ultimately, yourself into slavery might be your only remaining choice. The widow in today's passage has reached the point where her creditor was preparing to take the two children in lieu of the family's debt.

Clearly she feels that Elisha has some sense of responsibility for her family's well-being, and so she asks him to intervene.

In a story reminiscent of Elijah in 1 Kings 17:8–16, where God provides miraculously for a widow and her son, Elisha instructs the woman to gather as many vessels as possible and God provides an abundance of oil. Indeed, she has so much oil to sell that she will be able to settle her debts and live off the rest.

Julie Faith Parker directs our attention to the children in the story. Were they aware of why they were busily finding empty vessels from the neighbours? Were they only too aware of what was at stake? Whatever the case, the children 'unobtrusively pour themselves into the task at hand and thereby avoid slavery by doing what slaves must do'. She goes on to point out that they are the only figures in the Old Testament 'who proactively work on their own behalf to stave off enslavement' ('Valuable and vulnerable: children in the Hebrew Bible, especially in the Elisha cycle', Brown University, 2013, both quotes from p. 124).

We might describe this story as bittersweet. For this particular family, Elisha's involvement provides a way of rescue and demonstrates not only his prophetic credentials but also the power of God. But what of the many other families in similar straits?

# 4 Agents of change

In today's passage we read about a child who was both a victim and an agent of change. The main character of the story is Naaman, a great and accomplished Syrian general who is cured of a skin disease through an encounter with the prophet Elisha. While most of the story focuses on the (at times faulty and imprudent) attitudes and actions of adults, the entire episode hangs on the words of a trafficked child. This nameless young girl has been taken captive from her home in Israel by Syrian raiding parties and set to work for Naaman's wife. Knowing of his skin disease, the girl expresses a wish to her mistress that Naaman could be 'with' Israel's prophet, who would surely heal him of his disease. As the story unfolds, her word is taken seriously and this leads to Naaman encountering Elisha, being healed and having some kind of 'conversion' experience to faith in Yahweh – and all this because of the word of a powerless little girl who is forgotten as the story continues.

She is a nameless spoil of war, caught up in events far beyond her control: plundered from home and family, enslaved in an alien, enemy land. Who knows what has happened to her and many others like her?

Esther Menn suggests that this little girl points 'to the vulnerability of children of all ages, who are caught up in the violence and upset of communal or national conflicts' ('Child characters in biblical narratives', in Marcia J. Bunge, ed., *The Child in the Bible*, p. 351).

The story is sobering in the way that it depicts with almost brutally concise matter-of-factness the dire circumstances of the girl, yet at the same time exemplifies how God finds ways of bringing about his purposes through people in the most unpromising of circumstances. It doesn't lessen the pain or undermine her experiences. Rather, this story infuses her story with hope.

# 5 What does acceptable worship look like?

Israel's prophets had much to say about the relationship between Israel's covenant faithfulness and ethical life. As we've seen from, for example, the book of Deuteronomy, the vision of life in the land under God's rule didn't separate religious activity and devotion from relationships and responsibilities in society. One might even say that the latter was a 'litmus test' for the former.

Isaiah's opening prophecy is a case in point. It is a strong, stinging message from God concerning the state of Israel's relationship with him and the nature of true worship. It is also a rich introduction to many themes that will follow throughout this most stunning of biblical books.

The oracle opens with a call to creation to act as witnesses, as if God is bringing legal charges against Israel. They are like a wayward and rebellious child who despises their parents and their upbringing, or an ignorant beast who has no sense or understanding of their owner (vv. 2–4). In their stubborn rebellion they have endured all kinds of abuses and suffering (vv. 5–7; see Isaiah 36 for the circumstances around this desolation), yet in God's graciousness he has spared them from total destruction (vv. 8–9).

This most shocking of openings begs the question: what does such ignorance and rebellion look like? What has so enraged Israel's covenant God that he likens them to those archetypally wicked cities of Sodom and Gomorrah (v. 10)?

In verses 11–15 we are given a picture of ineffective worship that disgusts rather than delights God. The people are performing: they are bringing sacrifices and offerings; they are gathering together before God; they are observing certain special days and occasions; they are praying. But God cannot look upon their rituals without seeing their treatment of the poor and their denial of justice to the fatherless and the widow (vv. 15–17).

Because of their particular and intense vulnerabilities, the treatment of the widow and fatherless is a kind of spiritual barometer of Israel's true religious devotion and commitment to the covenant.

And herein lies Israel's hope: even now, Israel may choose to change their ways by seeking justice and correcting oppression, as proof of a renewed and genuine devotion to their God. Only then will their worship become acceptable.

# 6 Becoming angry

I was drawn to this passage a number of years ago by a student from East Africa who saw parallels between this psalm and the recruitment of child soldiers in his home context.

In the Hebrew Bible, Psalms 9 and 10 are presented as a single, acrostic poem (where each verse begins with a successive letter of the Hebrew alphabet). Psalm 9 calls on God to exert his rule over the nations, whereas Psalm 10 is a little closer to home.

The opening line asks God directly why he does nothing about the injustices going on in Israel. The wicked are arrogant, greedy and godless (vv. 2–4, 6, 11). They pursue and ensnare the vulnerable with manipulative schemes (vv. 2, 7–10). Notice the mini case study he includes in verses 8–10 of the wicked lurking with intent, picking off the weak and vulnerable, ensnaring them in his exploitative schemes.

The psalmist is in deep distress because he sees the wicked exploiting the vulnerable and giving no consideration of God's requirements or intent to judge their sin. We could even say that he is more angry with God for letting them get away with it than with the wicked themselves. Not only do they get away with it; they prosper (v. 5)!

A turning point appears in verse 12, where the psalmist calls on God to reassert his rule and act on behalf of the afflicted. Though it appears that God is not paying attention, the psalmist declares that the plots of the wicked are indeed under God's scrutiny and judgement (vv. 15–16). There will come a time when he will put things right. The fatherless will receive justice (vv. 17–18) and therefore may have hope as they entrust themselves to God.

# Guidelines

Over the course of this week's studies we have seen a variety of ways in which vulnerable children and young people feature in the pages of the Old Testament. Sometimes they are characters in narratives that demonstrate the world's brokenness. That they can be agents of change themselves, and not just passive recipients of actions done to them, is instructive. In the darkest of situations, God may use the unlikeliest of people. Might we even say that the narratives of Miriam or the Israelite servant girl illustrate that sometimes in God's purposes only the weak and the powerless can make the decisive difference?

That Israel's law addressed the plight of vulnerable children also shows us something of God's commitments. The pursuit of justice on behalf of the vulnerable is an indispensable part of the calling of God's people. The prophets knew this only too well; as Isaiah put it, how we treat the vulnerable is an indicator of how we really feel about God.

I hope we have also seen that scripture is not naive about the plight of the vulnerable. For every story of deliverance and provision, we are supposed to remember there were others without the happy ending. The psalms of lament, in particular, keep us attentive to the painful realities of life in our broken world. As well as intervening and pursuing justice for vulnerable young people, as well as sharing the news of God's kingdom with them, there is also a place to cry out to God with and for them.

As we saw, Psalm 10 confronts us with some of the wickedness evident in the world that me may prefer to ignore. It offers no easy answers, yet, without driving us to passivity, gives us hopeful language for our distress and the distress of others. It keeps us honest; it keeps us attentive.

**FURTHER READING**

Commentaries in the NIBC series: James Bruckner, *Exodus*; Christopher J.H. Wright, *Deuteronomy*; Iain Provan, *1 and 2 Kings*; John Goldingay, *Isaiah*.

Krish Kandiah with Miriam Kandiah, *Home for Good: Making a difference for vulnerable children*, updated edition (Hodder & Stoughton, 2017).

Elaine Storkey, *Scars across Humanity: Understanding and overcoming violence against women* (SPCK, 2015).

Home for Good: **homeforgood.org.uk**; thirtyone:eight: **thirtyoneeight.org**; The Children's Society: **childrenssociety.org.uk**; Viva – Together for Children: **viva.org**; World Vision: **worldvision.org.uk**.

# Interfaith engagement

Richard Martin

The second week in November each year is kept as Inter Faith Week. These notes highlight examples from the Bible of Jews and Christians engaging with people of other faiths, with a view to offering possibilities for such dialogue today. Of course, there are many more than we can cover in six days, but I hope they will enable you to look anew at your own context and to reflect how you may be called to respond to it.

A word about that context: I am not simply considering where you live. For some of us, people of other faiths are on our doorstep and have been for many years. For others, the local community may be still largely Christian/post-Christian. But when we go to a hospital, place of further education or prison or to work in any city, when we consider national politics, when we engage in any form of chaplaincy, we will find that we cannot escape the need to engage in a Christlike way with people of other faiths.

I have limited myself to examples of interfaith engagement in the UK, but this is a global issue and one with which Christians overseas have wrestled for many years: perhaps the doyen of them being Bishop Kenneth Cragg, whose scholarly book *The Call of the Minaret* was published in 1956. I am also aware that most of my examples are taken from Anglican sources, but much of this work is conducted ecumenically.

I have tried to keep these notes practical and so do not get immersed in the issue of salvation (who is saved, who – if anyone – isn't and how); in my experience that discussion generates more heat than light. 'Will not the Judge of all the earth do right?' (Genesis 18:25).

Bible quotations are taken from the NIV.

# 1 All religions contain diversity

**Acts 23:6–10**

Here is Paul rather cynically playing divide and rule in the Sanhedrin. There is a lovely comic moment in Luke's account when the Pharisees consider the possibility that a spirit or an angel has spoken to Paul, much to the annoyance, no doubt, of the Sadducees, who believe in neither. This cameo, though, has serious implications for interfaith engagement, for two reasons.

First, just as we now recognise that there was a wide diversity in the Judaism of Jesus and Paul's day, so also today faiths are not monochrome. When we embark on learning about other faiths, we are taught for example about the essentials of Islam (the five pillars), only to quickly discover that the Muslim community is divided between Sunni and Shi'ite and Sufi. There are also the Ahmadiyyas, who identify as Muslim but are regarded as unorthodox by the other groups. Such diversity of doctrine and practice can be found in every faith you will encounter.

Staying with Islam, this means that we have to be careful not to assume that the Muslim person we meet or the mosque we are invited to is in agreement with the one across the street. For example, Ahmadiyya Muslims are usually very keen on interfaith cooperation, but can be isolated from other Muslim groups. And, of course, within the members of any group there will be people who toe the party line to a greater and lesser extent. Statements like 'Muslims say…' are therefore usually too general. It is a mistake to try to fit people into a box. Rather, we should encounter each person in their uniqueness.

Second, and at the same time, the huge diversity within Christianity can lead to confusion in people of other faiths, about both doctrine and practice. The church is not monochrome either! It is worth remembering that the only Christian someone may have met was someone who aggressively tried to convert them – or even a Jehovah's Witness or a Mormon. Sometimes clearing up surprising misunderstandings can be the start of a fruitful conversation which acknowledges tolerance of difference within Christ's body while explaining its boundaries. In Paul's own day the outsider could have been forgiven for being confused about whether Christianity required its members to be circumcised. On that issue Paul opposed the Pharisee opinion, but here he sides with them against the Sadducees.

# 2 Scriptural reasoning

**Acts 17:28**

Paul's speech to the Athenians at the Areopagus (Acts 17:22–31) is remarkable for many reasons (for example, in contrast to his principles set out in 1 Corinthians 2:2, he mentions neither the cross nor Christ), but I have focused on verse 28, where he quotes from Greek poets, probably Epimenides and Aratus. Paul shows that he has read and reflected upon texts treasured by others and finds within them common ground which chimes with his understanding and explanation of his Christian faith.

The practice of scriptural reasoning follows Paul's practice. Simply put, it involves meeting with people of another faith and letting each other explain what their holy scriptures says about a chosen topic. It enables people who treasure their own scriptures to expound them, as long as they are then prepared to listen as others do the same. In recent years, the Cambridge Inter-Faith Programme has developed excellent resources to support scriptural reasoning, many of which are available online (albeit with a focus on meetings of Muslim, Jews and Christians).

In Gravesend a small group of Christians I have been part of, from various churches and denominations, have followed the example of John Parry – see *The Word of God is Not Bound* (CFCC, 2009) – in meeting a small group of Sikhs for scriptural reasoning. We agree a theme – recent examples being fasting, God and work – and settle on a place and date to meet. Then each faith group appoints someone to bring along printed copies of a passage from their holy book that relates to that theme. At the meeting one faith group explains what their passage says, and any necessary context, before inviting the other faith's members to make comments and ask questions. Then we swap over. It has proved illuminating and challenging and has enabled strong friendships to be built without in any way compromising each other's beliefs. However, it does happen that, like Paul, we find nuggets of common ground.

Readers of *Guidelines* are among those who treasure the Bible. Scriptural reasoning provides a framework in which to share its message, in a respectful way, with people of other faiths. The only proviso is that you offer them the courteous listening you experience. I commend it to you!

# 3 Accepting hospitality

**Luke 7:36–50**

How many times did Jesus offer hospitality? Not very often! Maybe the feeding of the 5,000 counts, and the last supper. How many times did he receive hospitality? There are many instances: in Mark's gospel alone he is a guest at Simon and Andrew's house (1:29–31), Levi's house (2:15), 'a house' (3:20), Jairus' house (5:38), 'the house' (7:17), a house in Tyre (7:24), a house in Capernaum (9:33), at Bethany (11:11–12; 14:3) and finally in Jerusalem (14:14).

Today's passage from Luke is another example of Jesus being a guest. In his wonderful book *Jesus through Middle Eastern Eyes* (SPCK, 2008), Kenneth Bailey offers a reading (pp. 239–60) that opens our eyes to the norms of hospitality Jesus was entitled to expect and to the degree of humiliation Simon heaps upon him by deliberately failing to observe them. Bailey argues that Simon was very rude to Jesus in front of all his other guests, and the woman seems to have been trying to redress the balance.

If I am host, I control the menu, the guest list, the seating plan, the speaking list and the timings. If I am a guest, I have to politely go along with my host's arrangements. Jesus seems to have preferred the risky business of being a guest to the power of being a host. That shouldn't surprise us. In this matter, as throughout his life on earth, he preferred humility to control, trust to certainty.

If we are seeking Christlike engagement with people of other faiths, it is good, therefore, to resist the temptation to invite them to come to us, and instead to accept what may be frequent invitations to be their guests. You will sometimes feel out of your comfort zone, you could be uncertain how to behave or you may find the food a little too spicy! But just by accepting, just by being there, you are emulating Christ's boundary-crossing mission. Unlike him, but like Francis when he visited the Sultan, venturing across the Crusade battle lines in Damietta in 1219, you will be welcomed and honoured.

# 4 Converting is complex

2 Kings 5 is another story with moments of humour: the diplomatic mission from Aram to Israel based on a little girl's simple faith (vv. 2–5), the neurotic response of the king of Israel (v. 7) the pomposity of Naaman (vv. 11–12) and Gehazi's pointless lies (v. 25). It is also a wonderful story of healing, and as Jesus points out on his preaching debut (Luke 4:27), it was a Gentile who is healed. Because of this blessing, Naaman decides to abandon the gods of Aram and to worship only the Lord (v. 15). It's a story too of interfaith conversion.

But read on. It's not so simple. Naaman still has to live at home in Aram, under authority. This will mean compromise – specifically, bowing down to Rimmon in the temple when his master does so. Is that okay? What would you say? What does Elisha say? Perhaps surprisingly, he agrees. In Rimmon's temple, Naaman's devotion to Yahweh can remain secret.

This leads to several principles for interfaith work today.

First, Naaman volunteers to change his religious allegiance. No one asks him to, or suggests that he ought to, in response to his healing. Blessing others with the love of God comes without strings attached.

Second, there is an awareness of the deep cost of conversion. It is very often a decision that if it were made public would mean not just leaving a faith, but also a community and maybe also one's family and support network. Therefore, when someone wishes to remain a secret Christian within their original context, our judgements must be very gentle, like Elisha's.

Third, if someone does change their faith community allegiance, however desirable that may seem to the receiving community, it is important to acknowledge the sense of betrayal by the community the person has left. If we are tempted to celebrate people coming from another faith to Christianity, we should reflect on how we would feel if one of our young people became a Buddhist, for example. This understanding can shape our interfaith dialogue.

Naaman's story is echoed today. People do change faith. But the experience of doing so is rarely clean-cut.

# 5 Working (and praying?) together for the common good

**Jeremiah 29:4–7**

Interfaith engagement does not have to focus on faith!

If dialogue is to move on from accepting and offering hospitable friendship, for real cooperation to be established, it will usually need an outside focus, a project or issue that is of concern to all.

There are many issues around which different faiths can gather and on which they can work together. Examples include concern for the environment (traced back to Pope John Paul II's interfaith peace conference at Assisi in 1986), homelessness and countering extremism. Food poverty could be tackled through the coordinated provision of langar at a gurdwara and soup kitchens. Money could be given by one faith community to support the project of another faith: in Gravesend in 2018 the Sikh community cancelled their Diwali firework display and gave the budget to the local Trussell Trust food bank. Or there could be a local political issue to campaign on together, such as a new road or funding services for the elderly.

Jeremiah urges the exiles, newly arrived in Babylon, to make common cause with those already there who seek its peace and prosperity. In contrast to the Jonahs, who would be delighted if God destroyed the whole place, they should work for its welfare, because that is what God wills. Jeremiah also urges them to pray to God for the city. The Babylonians would have been praying to their gods for the same place. They did not pray together, but their prayers had a common petition.

To what extent should we pray alongside people of other faiths today? Most Christians will not feel able to pray the words other faiths use, but there may be opportunity to attend the worship of another faith and pray silently our own prayers there. A less controversial practice might occur after an atrocity, where a vigil may be held, at which all those attending pray silently in their own way. Whether a member of another faith can be invited to pray in their way in a Christian place of worship needs much discernment and sensitivity (and in the case of the Church of England, it is forbidden under Canon Law).

Whatever our approach to shared prayer, it is worth remembering that prayers for peace, justice and the environment (to name but three examples) are not the sole prerogative of Christians.

# 6 Experiencing God in unexpected places

**Genesis 28:10–17**

At Bethel, Jacob, to his surprise, meets God. It has certainly been my experience that God can draw close to me in unfamiliar locations, including the places of worship of other faiths: a Buddhist temple in London, a Hindu mandir in Neasden, a mosque in Birmingham and a synagogue in Chatham, to name but four.

Visiting another faith's place of worship can be approached just as a cultural or fact-finding exercise. But believers in an omnipresent God will be open to the spiritual there too.

This principle can be extended to any expression of interfaith dialogue. In engaging with people, practices and scriptures of other faiths, our appreciation of our own faith can be broadened, enhanced and deepened, if we are open to the possibility that God can speak to us and meet us there.

Sometimes God might challenge our practice, which may seem half-hearted when compared with the devotion of others (e.g. Muslim fasting in Ramadan), but just as often he will encourage us with a new insight into his holiness, grace and wisdom – endless riches to be discovered – or into human nature.

Let one story illustrate this. One day we were discussing with our Sikh friends ways in which God enters a human heart. We referred to Revelation 3:20: 'If anyone… opens the door I will come in.' The Sikh reply was that the Guru Granth Sahib speaks of doors to the body and a gate to the heart. The seven doors or orifices of the body need to have their appetites tamed (not extinguished) before God can gain access to the gate of the heart. That seemed a very helpful way of understanding Paul's teaching about the relationship between flesh and spirit (Romans 6:11).

Interfaith engagement opens up a wealth of new understanding. It is good for us!

# Guidelines

I hope this week's readings and comments have whetted your appetite for interfaith engagement and that you have been moved to seek ways of taking this forward. Here are some ideas:

- Go on to the internet and see if there is a local interfaith council. If so, make contact with the secretary and go along to a meeting.
- Buy and read one of the books on the 'Further reading' list or visit one of the websites there.
- Ask a young person to tell you what they are studying at school in religious studies, and how they feel about it.
- Talk to a chaplain about how faiths work together in a secular setting.
- Find out if anyone in your church works alongside people of other faiths, and talk about the conversations they have.
- If you have neighbours of another faith, ask if they will show you around their place of worship.
- Or just take courage and go there by yourself. (If you cannot, go online and take a virtual tour.)
- But above all, make contact, make conversation, make friendships! And may God bless you.

---

**FURTHER READING**

Ray Gaston, *Faith, Hope and Love: Interfaith engagement as practical theology* (SCM, 2017).

Andrew Smith, *Vibrant Christianity in Multifaith Britain: Equipping the church for a faithful engagement with people of different faiths* (BRF, 2018).

Tom Wilson, *Hospitality, Service, Proclamation: Interfaith engagement as Christian discipleship* (SCM, 2019).

Examples of interfaith engagement in the UK can be found at **churchofengland. org/about/work-other-faiths/about-presence-engagement**. There are also many examples at **interfaith.org.uk/activity**.

# Daniel

Bill Goodman

Who has real power and what does that look like? Is resistance futile – or can it show the impotence of certain kinds of power? Does history have a shape and purpose which we can discern? These kinds of questions deserve attention – and these are the concerns of the book of Daniel.

The book fascinates and sometimes bewilders readers, not least in its diversity. In the first half, colourful characters inhabit entertaining, inspirational stories of intrigue and conflict in the imperial court. This leads on to spectacular but cryptic apocalyptic visions awash with symbolic language, which have been used by later readers (from Jesus' day to our own) to make sense of current events and to reassure people who feel uncertain and anxious about the future.

The diversity in the book of Daniel prompts debate about what kind of writing this is: in Christian Bibles it is found among the prophets, while the Jewish canon has it as part of the 'writings', alongside the wisdom books. Further questions are raised by the language used: why does the book begin in Hebrew, then switch early in chapter 2 into the related language of Aramaic – only for Hebrew to resume for the final five chapters?

The book depicts specific historical events: the enforced exile of the Jerusalem elite in Babylon after 597BC and the subsequent rise and fall of particular rulers (chapters 1—6); then much later events around 164BC, when the reign of the Seleucid king Antiochus Epiphanes brought terror and trauma to the people of Jerusalem and Judea (chapters 7—12). So was the whole book completed during the exile in Babylon – with the dream-visions glimpsing crises in the far distant future? Or was it finally completed centuries later, by a writer who was looking back on recent traumatic events (but framing them in a forward-looking prophetic style)? Many scholars now accept a later date as most likely, particularly because of the degree of detail in the visions. Either way, the book's messages about power and God working in history are profoundly relevant for us today.

Bible quotations are taken from the NRSV. Author references are to works in the 'Further reading' list.

# 1 Perceptions of power

The first character we meet seems overwhelmingly powerful: King Nebuchad-nezzar of Babylon. His all-conquering army has defeated the forces of Judea, removing the Jerusalem elite to avoid future rebellion. Returning to his royal court, he exercises power of life and death over captive exiles and his own people alike, intimidating even his trusted officials (v. 10).

And yet… even those officials can be won over and persuaded to bend the rules (vv. 11–14). The mighty king can be subverted and disobeyed, provided his minions can keep him in the dark. (And those officials probably do quite well out of it, with the rejected rich food and wine left at their disposal!) In a first glimpse of the wry humour with which the book is laced, we see the king contentedly oblivious to what has really happened (vv. 18–20).

Daniel and his friends seem powerless; even their names are taken from them and new ones imposed on them – this conquering culture seeks to reconfigure their very identity. Yet they choose to ask: 'What does being faith-ful to my God in this foreign land require of me?' That question leads them to discover their own power by making a stand: the issue they choose relates to food and drink (perhaps eating the king's food meant expressing loyalty to him as provider). The book's understated humour emerges again in the final verse (v. 21): Daniel eventually lives so long, he outlasts Nebuchadnezzar and his successors and the whole Babylonian empire! Who would have bet on that?

Behind Daniel and his friends stands the ultimate power. Their God is the one who 'gives', a verb used three times in this chapter: God gives Jerusalem into the hands of the Babylonians, rather than Nebuchadnezzar's own power (v. 2); God gives Daniel and his friends favour in the eyes of the officials, rather than their own persuasiveness (v. 9); God gives them knowledge, wisdom and insight, rather than the distinguished education they receive (v. 17).

God subverts human perceptions of power. Down the centuries, Daniel has provided inspiration for people resisting oppression, including Jews in medi-eval Germany refusing enforced conversion and baptism by the Crusaders and, more recently, South African Christians calling for civil disobedience against the apartheid regime. What kind of inspiration does Daniel offer for today's world?

## 2  The revealer of mysteries

**Daniel 2:1–23**

'Knowledge is power' declares a popular saying, attributed to Francis Bacon and appropriated by others since. In Daniel 2 we see how knowledge can give power – and how God-given insight is also needed in the process of developing wisdom.

Powerful people can be surprisingly vulnerable, troubled in their minds and emotions. King Nebuchadnezzar provides an example of this – and of how insecurity can prompt fits of rage, erratic behaviour and unreasonable demands. Why does he not recount his dream? Has he simply forgotten the details, as sometimes happens, yet woken up with a conviction that the dream disturbed him? Or does he deliberately withhold this information in order to challenge his array of expert advisors, to see if they are really credible, not just making stuff up? Perhaps he fears conspiracy or manipulation: if he believes his advisors and acts accordingly, they will be exercising a degree of power over him (v. 9). He cannot rule alone – yet who can he really trust?

As the fallout from these perilous power struggles descends on the wider court, Daniel (with his life on the line) promises to sort out the crisis, displaying a degree of trust which could seem naive: faith in the effectiveness of prayer, in his friends and above all in his God. They pray, and their faith is rewarded. While others shrug their shoulders at the remoteness and inaccessibility of the gods (v. 11), Daniel and his friends request compassion from 'the God of heaven' (v. 18; see also vv. 37, 44). From the heavenly realms their God sees everything that is going on – and makes things happen. This God 'changes times and seasons', moving history from one epoch to another – which may include sweeping away kings and empires to replace them with new ones (v. 21). This God chooses to reveal mysteries (vv. 19, 22, 28, 29, 47): disclosing more fully truths about the future which up to now have been partially hidden. This God gives understanding and wisdom to a faithful servant – gifts that suddenly bring this vulnerable young exile an opportunity to exercise power (vv. 20–23). Having received this power, how will Daniel make use of it?

# 3 Can the high and mighty learn?

**Daniel 2:24–49**

Daniel's first steps into local politics show a striking lack of concern for building his own ego or his own little empire. He saves not just his own life, but also the lives of his future rivals, the king's established advisors (v. 24). He resists the temptation to hype up his own abilities and wisdom, simply pointing to God as the one who chooses to reveal mysteries to the king through him (vv. 27–30). Like Joseph in the court of Pharaoh (Genesis 41, a passage with various similarities to this one), Daniel offers directness, transparency and integrity, which carry conviction: here is someone the king can find 'trustworthy' (v. 45).

Nebuchadnezzar's dream of an awesome colossus which is ultimately smashed, turned to dust and blown away is a vivid declaration of the transience of kings and their empires. Despite their impressive appearance, an inherent instability threatens them. 'Feet of clay' is another phrase we sometimes hear today, drawn from this passage in Daniel. Individuals and whole political systems can look strong and impressive yet have an underlying weakness which we may not have noticed – a weakness which leads ultimately to their downfall.

Down the centuries different readers have often mapped this biblical passage on to the regimes of their day, either to support or to critique their own rulers. Scholars today agree that the statue in Daniel 2 depicts four ancient kingdoms/empires: either the Babylonians, Medes, Persians and Greeks or the Babylonians, Medo-Persians, Greeks and Romans.

But then what is the 'stone' (vv. 34–35)? This ultimate king or kingdom, which has power to pulverise human empires, morphs into a 'great mountain'; the language here evokes Israel's God, the 'rock' (e.g. Deuteronomy 32:4; Isaiah 44:8; 51:1), whose glory fills the earth (Isaiah 6:3). But how does this ultimate, divine kingdom finally appear? Christians have traditionally seen this in the arrival of Jesus Christ (Matthew 21:42, 44; Romans 9:33). However, the New Testament writers reframe the picture from Daniel in terms of an unexpectedly hidden kingdom, developing gradually and to be revealed in all its power and glory only at Christ's second coming (e.g. Matthew 13:24–43).

As in chapter 1, we see that God is the one who gives power as God chooses (vv. 37–38). If human rulers abuse the sovereignty delegated to them by the God of heaven, God may choose to revoke divine generosity and take back control. All must bow to the ultimate 'Lord of kings' (v. 47).

# 4 Who is the God that will deliver you?

The book's comic element re-emerges, presenting cartoonish caricatures: a ridiculously vast idol, an over-elaborate bunch of dignitaries, fanfares from an over-sized band; the mighty king contorted with rage, overheating a furnace to such an absurd extent that his own obedient minions get roasted – and in the middle of it all, the three heroes miraculously keeping their cool when the heat really is on, ultimately rewarded with promotion rather than incineration! Humour and laughter are well-proven ways to puncture pomposity and cut the mighty down to size.

But this satirical humour is bittersweet: it depicts the kind of injustice and violence by which Jewish people (and others) have suffered and died down the years and continue to suffer and die in our own day. We sense that this is no laughing matter; yet laughter can be a declaration of hope and defiance.

Shadrach, Meshach and Abednego's response to the king's order suggests ambivalence: they seem to sense that their God can save them, but cannot be sure that this will happen (vv. 17–18). God is not at the beck and call of human beings (like Aladdin's genie), existing to do their will. Experience indicates that God does not usually perform this kind of miracle; there is no promise in the passage that God will miraculously intervene to save other people in similar positions.

The king's education continues. His power, displayed by the obedience of vast crowds, turns out to be limited: he can threaten violent execution, but he cannot actually force anyone to worship the huge statue. His wild rage is a response to discovering the limits of his power: realising that he cannot control everything prompts him to lose his self-control.

The king needs to see things more clearly, and we find ourselves looking through his eyes. Who is the mysterious fourth figure he sees in the blazing furnace (v. 25)? The Old Greek translation provides extra detail, taking us into the furnace, where we hear prayers and encounter an angel (as Daniel will later in his own great escape, 6:22).

The opening chapter of this book explored accommodation: it seemed that those living under imperial rule might thrive and prosper even while preserving a godly lifestyle. But from now onwards we find a growing critique of the oppressive arrogance of despotic power and a call to resist it.

# 5  Can the high and mighty change?

Haven't we been here before? Again a dream to interpret, again this great king is cut down to size. If this series of short stories forms a continuous narrative, he seems to be a slow learner! Or perhaps here Nebuchadnezzar – the king who destroyed the Jerusalem temple – is an archetype, representing a succession of mighty kings who oppressed ancient Israel, leaving wounds in the collective memory which needed healing.

This time, the mighty king narrates the opening and closing sections, giving his own testimony: a personal account of being humiliated, transformed and restored. This time, he remembers his dream and recounts it. Unusually, we are told Daniel's emotional response: the dream alarms him (v. 19). One aspect of Daniel's transparent integrity is his honesty: he tells what he sees, even if it feels risky. (Perhaps the king's other advisors also grasped the meaning of the dream but were afraid of telling him, in case it triggered his anger.) The king affirms Daniel's honesty, realising that he needs advisors who are truthful.

The dream depicts royal greatness as potentially beneficial: those who have power should use it to empower those who are vulnerable, providing food and security (v. 21). But the temptation to self-aggrandising arrogance leads to some kind of mental illness and divinely sanctioned humiliation (vv. 28–33). He needs to submit to 'the Most High' (the distinctive name for Daniel's God in this chapter – 4:2, 17, 34, etc.), the one who has ultimate sovereignty, even over human kings (vv. 24, 32, 34).

When the time of Nebuchadnezzar's judgement has gone on long enough, God gives grace, restoring him to sanity and power. This enables him to respond by giving worship and testimony to 'the King of heaven' (v. 37). It does seem that Nebuchadnezzar has finally learned some humility: he becomes human again, apparently redeemed as well as restored.

Did the events depicted in these chapters really happen? Some readers feel it is essential to understand the stories literally, lest they lose credibility. Others hear them as more like Jesus' parables – does it matter whether the prodigal son, for example, is a genuine historical character? Either way, we need to make sure we get the point of each story and are open to receive its encouragement and challenge.

# 6 Weighed and found wanting

**Daniel 5**

Even the high and mighty are mortal. Nebuchadnezzar's days have ended. In what ways will subsequent kings be similar or different? Here Belshazzar is deliberately contrasted with his predecessor, the repentant Nebuchadnezzar, referred to as his father. (Other historical records indicate that Belshazzar's actual father was Nabonidus, who took the throne by force but then spent many years in Arabia, leaving his son as regent in his place. Thus Belshazzar was Nebuchadnezzar's effective successor.)

As in previous chapters, we find an unexpected mystery, more useless advisors and God's servant needed to make sense of it all. There are also a few more comic details: the mighty king turning deathly pale, with knees knocking and possibly a humiliating moment of incontinence (v. 6, translation uncertain); and the arrival of the queen (or perhaps the queen mother – someone old and wise enough to remember times past), who has to come in, restore some decorum and indicate a way out of this chaos (v. 10)!

Daniel, who was generally courteous to Nebuchadnezzar, is abrupt with Belshazzar, like a prophet bringing a word of judgement (v. 17). He uncovers subtle word plays in the enigmatic divine graffiti, revealing hidden levels of meaning contained in it. The message is that Belshazzar is a lightweight, lacking any real substance: 'powerful, yet pathetic' (Pace, p. 160). He is condemned for his arrogance, blasphemy and worship of idols; the list of materials used to make idols emphasises that they are simply human constructions, with no real life in them (vv. 4, 23). By contrast, the true, living God, 'the Most High' (v. 21), is also the one 'in whose power is your very breath' (v. 23); he may allow Belshazzar's breath to be literally taken away.

Even when the writing is on the wall (another phrase from this book which has found its way into our language), Belshazzar's response is not to learn from Nebuchadnezzar's example and repent; Belshazzar seems to shrug off the personal challenge. Then he is killed that very night (perhaps by his own people). If he helped his father attain the kingship through the violence of a palace coup, then his own demise in similar fashion seems ironically appropriate. The high and mighty can be strangely insecure.

# Guidelines

- Think about areas in life where you have some degree of power. There may be more than you realise! It might be in how you handle family relationships; in the life of your local church; in your workplace; in the local community; in decisions you make about spending your time and money. Is pride sometimes too tempting, or the desire to control and dominate? Are there power struggles developing, which need to be handled differently? What is there in this week's readings that might shed light on that?

- Daniel and his three friends are given new Babylonian names, yet also retain their Hebrew names. 'The double names are an index of the double identities experienced by all exiles, immigrants, and colonised peoples, who must continually negotiate the sometimes-conflicting claims of the two cultures to which they belong' (Newsom, p. 48). Does this experience of conflicting identities resonate with you? What about other people you know? Which are proving to be the most effective ways for you and others to navigate this kind of tension?

- Being different in the ways you think, speak, dress or behave can cause offence to others among whom you live. They may feel challenged by your unwillingness to live by common conventions and expectations and may feel you are questioning their views. How does this kind of tension play out in your experience? In what ways shall we choose to resist assimilation into the dominant culture which surrounds us?

- The arrival of the Covid-19 crisis in 2020 was a shock, particularly to many who had felt powerful. Systems and structures in politics and economics which had seemed entrenched and reliable were suddenly undermined, even swept aside. Our world was brought low – by a microscopic virus! How did you experience that? Did it change your feelings and understanding about who has real power and how that power should best be used in future?

- The power of stories and storytellers (and other artists) is often feared by oppressive regimes, because storytellers can empower people to see the world differently. In what ways do these stories in the book of Daniel prompt you to imagine a different kind of world to the one we live in today? Are you willing to start creating that world and living in it – whatever the cost?

# 1 Thrown to the lions

**Daniel 6**

Empires rise and fall; now the Babylonian one has been superseded. But the lure of power-politics continues: anyone who does well and demonstrates integrity needs to watch out, lest jealous, manipulative rivals seek to stab them in the back.

Connections are emerging between these chapters. We saw how the king in chapter 5 was contrasted with the previous king in chapter 4. Now, in chapter 6, we find similarities which invite comparison with chapter 3: in both we meet malicious schemers seeking to destroy the innocent and godly hero(es), leading to rescue from an overwhelmingly dangerous situation by the living God through the intervention of an angel, with the true God acclaimed by the astonished king as a result. But there are contrasts as well: in chapter 6, the king fervently desires that his own command may somehow be thwarted and Daniel saved. Both kings discover limits to their power: Nebuchadnezzar is unable to kill Daniel's three friends, while Darius fails in his attempt to find a way to save Daniel.

Other historical sources make no mention of 'Darius the Mede' (5:31) – but they do highlight 'Darius the Persian', who ruled some years later (and facilitated rebuilding of the Jerusalem temple). The Darius we meet in Daniel 6 seems well-intentioned but weak, lacking the shrewdness needed in the political world. Officially he has absolute power, but his gullibility and weakness for flattery can be manipulated by his scheming and eventually bullying advisors. This king values Daniel, seems fond of him and clearly has a conscience (vv. 18–20); but he gets outmanoeuvred by his underlings. However, his final decree (after Daniel's miraculous escape) requires that universal recognition and deep reverence be shown to Daniel's God, rounding off this series of stories (vv. 25–27).

These ancient narratives have shown an enduring power. Remains of ancient synagogues and churches unearthed by archaeologists show how Daniel's escape from the lions brought comfort and inspiration to early Christians who faced harassment or persecution and to Jews facing persecution from authorities claiming to be Christian. Daniel's resistance to oppressive power is also prominent in some medieval Muslim traditions. More recently,

Mahatma Gandhi cited Daniel as an example of 'satyagraha', the essence of his nonviolent resistance to the rule of the British empire.

# 2 Murderous monsters and an everlasting kingdom

**Daniel 7**

Without warning, we return to the surreal world of dreams and visions: but from now on Daniel himself is the one who experiences them, is troubled by them (vv. 15, 28) and requires an interpreter. He becomes the narrator of the rest of the book.

The concentric structure which we glimpsed earlier emerges again, linking Daniel 2—7, the parts of the book written in Aramaic. We noted connections between Daniel 4 and 5 and between Daniel 3 and 6. Now in chapter 7, we find strong echoes of chapter 2 – but with the four empires of Nebuchadnezzar's dream reconfigured into four immense and powerful creatures.

Once again we find similarities and also contrasts between the two chapters. The fourth creature Daniel sees in chapter 7 does not show the vulnerability of the equivalent 'feet of clay' in chapter 2. In addition, it is succeeded by a 'small horn' – a further arrogant king, of whom we shall hear more in the chapters that follow. Ultimately all these regimes are succeeded by a human-like figure (literally 'one like a son of man'), to whom all sovereignty is given (vv. 13–14). Later explanation indicates that this figure represents 'the people of the holy ones of the Most High' (v. 27): God is on the side of God's people and will vindicate them. Christians and Jews have seen here a further overflow of meaning, a prophetic glimpse of a coming Messiah. In the New Testament we see Jesus as the 'Son of Man' (Mark 14:62; Revelation 1:7, 13). In this understanding, Jesus represents his people – he personifies the true Israel.

Against the odds, in the mid-second century BC the Jews did finally manage to throw off foreign rule, through the Maccabean revolt; they stayed free for a century, until the Romans invaded. This rebellion turned out not to be the ultimate, everlasting victory of the people of Yahweh described here (v. 27); it was more like the first instalment of an ultimate fulfilment, yet to come.

Attempts to describe God's appearance are rare in the Bible. Daniel offers a glimpse of one who seems timeless ('ancient'), seated in judgement, emanating purity, brilliance, mobility and a dangerous, transcendent otherness (enthroned amid 'fiery flames'), with countless attendants underlining the awesome royal splendour (vv. 9–10).

While this chapter links to the previous ones, it also forms a bridge to those that remain: Daniel will see further apocalyptic visions as the rest of the book unfolds.

# 3  How strong are the invincible?

**Daniel 8**

In another surreal vision, more bullying beasts appear. Yet the same period of history is in view. Babylon is muscled aside by the Medes and Persians; then more macho-male dominance brings the frenetic Greek goat, led by the 'great horn' of Alexander the Great – who suddenly dies at the height of his power (v. 8). Now his vast empire (which includes Judea) is carved up, with four of his generals fighting for control. The ironies of power are unveiled: kings and emperors who have seemed so invincible prove brittle and transient, collapsing with bewildering suddenness.

The 'little horn' which we first glimpsed in the previous chapter (7:8, 20–22) now emerges more clearly. The Seleucid King Antiochus IV styles himself 'Epiphanes', which means 'God Manifest' – a provocative blasphemy in the eyes of the people of the 'beautiful land' of Judea (v. 9), one of the areas he rules. The unruly Judahite leaders try scheming against him with the Egyptians; eventually Antiochus imposes direct rule, bringing violent disruption (vv. 11–12). He bans regular worship in the Jerusalem temple, replacing it with pagan worship; this is enforced for over three years (v. 14; compare 7:25).

But then what? The apocryphal books 1 and 2 Maccabees include vivid and colourful accounts of the ensuing revolt: the reconquest of Jerusalem and rededication of the temple by Judah the Maccabee (164BC), with Antiochus suddenly dying around the same time. There is no sign of these tumultuous events in the book of Daniel. The author of Daniel (whether looking ahead to the future or writing later and looking back on recent events) would surely have included restoration of worship in the temple if it had recently happened; instead, looking ahead, our author trusts that this, too, will come, in God's time.

Repeated phrases in the text emphasise how each of these empires and rulers seemed awesome in their day. But Daniel's visions give assurance that

God stands above them, sometimes achieving things through them, always ready to step in if they go too far. The visions also give power to Daniel himself: the sage is able to see the reality behind appearances and can share it with other people, as he does in what is recorded here.

# 4 Discerning God in the past, present and future

Embedded in the sequence of visions we find a stirring, heartfelt prayer. Daniel the exile is depicted here being enlightened about the future, glimpsing the traumatic events of the Antiochus crisis centuries later, as he pours out his repentance and pleads insistently with God.

How can Daniel repent of sins done by other people, some his contemporaries and others long dead (vv. 6, 16)? False guilt can be a destructive burden which should not be embraced. Yet all of us need to acknowledge our inheritance. As a UK citizen today, I enjoy the comforts of a wealthy society – comforts and wealth initially developed by previous generations, some of it through exploitation of colonies, the brutality of slavery and a disregard for the destruction of the wider environment. So I am implicated in the decisions of my ancestors, benefitting from their mistakes and sins as well as their work and wisdom.

Daniel recognises that each generation, including his own, is flawed. He and his people need to cast themselves on God's mercy, not presume on God's grace – and he finds assurance that he is 'greatly beloved' (vv. 23; 10:11, 19). He appeals to Yahweh's compassion and faithfulness, along with the importance of Yahweh's honour and reputation, which is bound up with the city and people who 'bear your name' (vv. 18–19).

Daniel is depicted trying to make sense of what God is doing in the light of what God has previously said. Through Jeremiah, God promised that the exile would be over in a lifetime (70 years – Jeremiah 29:10–14). Gabriel, Daniel's angelic guide, reworks Jeremiah's proclamations to find a further meaning; he uses seven, the symbolic number of completeness, in broad terms which may be approximate rather than precise. The first waves of returning exiles did indeed reach Jerusalem within 70 years and the city was then rebuilt with its worship re-established (v. 25). Yet much later (62 x 7 years after that return) the people of Jerusalem would face a crisis as bad as any that their ancestors had known, with the anointed high priest (Onias III) killed and the worship of Antiochus' pagan gods brought into Yahweh's temple (vv. 26–27). Gabriel affirms the appalling nature of that crisis – but also declares the time limit which God has set for it. When 70 x 7 years from the beginning of the exile are completed, disaster will overwhelm Antiochus (v. 24).

# 5 The end of the world as we know it?

**Daniel 10:1–19; 11:20–35**

The last three chapters of Daniel bring one final, very detailed vision, deepening the revelation given in chapter 8. Once again we find vivid imagery, symbolism and rhetoric which trigger our imagination, as do the ambiguities and puzzling details in these apocalyptic visions.

In the gospels, Jesus uses Daniel's phrasing to describe turmoil soon to devastate Jerusalem (Mark 13:14, 26). John, the author of Revelation, was a later visionary who looked at his world through lenses honed by the Old Testament – tinted particularly with Ezekiel and Daniel. John's vision of Christ the Son of Man (Revelation 1:12–20) has clear echoes of Daniel 10:5–6, 10–11. John sees in the oppressive Roman empire of his day such brutality that it combines Daniel's four monstrous empires, plus the 'little horn' (7:1–8), all rolled into one ultimate mega-monster (Revelation 13:1–10).

Centuries later, Martin Luther mapped Daniel's monsters and 'little horn' (combined with the idea of an 'antichrist') on to the power politics of his day, seeing in them oppression by the Pope, then later also Islam and invading Ottoman forces. During the English Civil War, Puritan forces applied the image of the 'little horn' to King Charles I, in order to justify beheading him. Meanwhile in our own times, Christian fundamentalists have variously identified the European Union, Barack Obama and Vladimir Putin in similar terms, while radical Muslim preachers have seen Israel as the 'little horn' and the victorious 'Son of Man' in Daniel 7:13 as representing Mohammed. The symbolic numbering of days, weeks and years found in Daniel 7—12 has also been mapped on to current crises and used to predict the imminent arrival of the Messiah.

So can we appropriate these times and visions however we choose? In light of the above, caution is advisable. Any reading of Daniel (or Revelation) which ignores their references to the politics of the author's own day is surely missing the point and abusing the intention of the text. But in addition, we may sometimes find a prophetic overflow of meaning which critiques other regimes beyond the author's day and shows repeated patterns in history. Using puzzling details in these texts to devise ingenious, specific timelines for our current crises invariably proves faulty. But these passages can furnish our imaginations with alternative visions of how the world really is, as well as how it could be and one day finally will be – inspiring us to work towards that transformation.

# 6 End in sight (and beyond)

**Daniel 11:36—12:13**

If there are recurring patterns to be discerned in political history, then repeated themes among the details of this long final vision may give us glimpses of them. Again and again we see here deception and intrigue, the urge to control, self-aggrandising macho men obsessed with achieving dominance, the destructive cost of their warfare, enriching of elites, lack of concern for justice and arrogant overreach by rulers who seem invincible – just before their sudden demise. All the while, mention of (let alone submission to) the ultimate King of kings is notable by its absence.

As we have seen, some readers today think the author of Daniel lived around the time of the exile in Babylon and was looking to a far-distant future, while others see him writing much later, during the crisis of the 160s BC, looking back on past events but writing in the style of a prediction. Either way, in this final part of the book, the writer does look to the future and predicts what is yet to come (11:40–45) – above all, the abrupt 'end' of Antiochus while at the height of his power (11:45).

The exact historical details of Antiochus' demise and sudden death are unclear; the books of Maccabees preserve various traditions about this. But the fulfilment of this prediction, along with the restoration of worship in the Jerusalem temple by the Maccabean rebels, are probably major reasons why the visions of Daniel were preserved: they were recognised as genuinely from God. They indicated that the chaos and bloodshed which the people of Judah lived through was not simply random; God had been watching over it and working through it.

Daniel seems to expect these events to bring in the end of history as we know it, including the raising of the dead for divine judgement – a rare glimpse of life after death in an Old Testament text (12:2–3, 13). Yet he is also told that no human can know when this final end of history will arrive (12:8–9). These visions both reveal and conceal. The demise of Antiochus will prove to be a foretaste of God's ultimate purpose, a glimpse of that final fulfilment – which will arrive afterwards, in due time (12:13).

## Guidelines

- Reflect on the various titles ascribed to the living God in this book, such as 'King of heaven', 'God of gods', 'Lord of lords', 'great God', 'living God', 'Most High' and 'Ancient One'. Yet this same God is not simply remote, but is also presented as 'our God', 'my God', 'your God', the God of the covenant, compassionate and forgiving, the one who hears prayer. How does all this inform your own understanding and relationship with God?

- What do you particularly notice about the way Daniel prays in chapters 2, 6 and 9? Reflect on those passages and see if his example can help you in any way to develop your own approach to prayer.

- Apocalyptic visions, such as those found in Daniel and Revelation, tend to trigger our imagination and our emotions. Richard Bauckham argues that part of their purpose is to challenge the perception of reality which we are used to, revealing its delusional aspects, and to furnish the imagination with 'prophetic counter-images', an alternative reality for us to explore and inhabit. Do any particular passages or images in the book of Daniel impact you in that way? What do these vivid images and symbols evoke in you?

- Daniel's visions repeatedly depict the global status quo of his day being suddenly disrupted in ways that previously seemed unimaginable. How does that speak to the experiences you have lived through, particularly during recent years? Does Daniel's conviction about God still being in control and working in history seem fanciful, or does it have an authentic ring in our day? If your answer is 'a bit of both', you might like to reflect on how you are handling that tension and how you help others handle it.

- What have you particularly learned from this book about good and bad ways to exercise power? Think again about your own roles and relationships in family, church, community, workplace and the wider world. What might you want to do differently in future? How might you encourage and challenge other people to use power differently, in matters that are close to home and also in wider, global concerns?

**FURTHER READING**

Greg Beale and Benjamin Gladd, *Hidden But Now Revealed: A biblical theology of mystery* (IVP Academic, 2014).

John Goldingay, *Daniel*, revised edition (Zondervan, 2015).

John Goldingay, *Daniel and the Twelve Prophets for Everyone* (SPCK, 2016).

Carol Newsom with Brennon Breed, *Daniel: A commentary* (Westminster John Knox Press, 2014).

Sharon Pace, *Daniel* (Smyth and Helwys, 2008).

Christopher J.H. Wright, *Hearing the Message of Daniel: Sustaining faith in today's world* (Eerdmans, 2017).

# Revelation 12—22: drawing back the curtain

## Stephen Finamore

Recent research into the book of Revelation draws our attention to the group of people that John calls 'my brothers the prophets'. Some writers think that the author shared his visions and his understanding of them with these colleagues and that when he had written them down in a book, they took responsibility for going around the churches, reading out the text and helping the churches to interpret it. This set of studies imagines that we are present to hear John introduce the final version of his book to his fellow prophets, to instruct them on its meaning and to send them out to the churches to teach the contents.

Bible quotations are taken from the NRSV.

## A message from John

Lots of you will know this already, but it won't hurt you to be reminded. Others of you are new and you need to hear this because it forms the foundation for everything else. Here are the seven – appropriately! – keys to understanding and teaching the book. Keep these in mind and you will serve the churches well.

1. Jesus gave me an apocalypse. This means an unveiling or a revelation. The visions are intended to show things that are currently hidden, in whole or in part, from us and from the world of our day. Your job is to pull back the curtain so that the churches see things as they truly are. You will show them the hidden spiritual realities that are at work in the world.

2. Most of the action takes place in – or is seen from the standpoint of – heaven; and heaven is God's temple. This temple used to have an earthly counterpart, or shadow, in Jerusalem. Like the one in Jerusalem, the heavenly true temple has, among other things, a Holy Place and a Holy of Holies. The heavenly Holy of Holies is God's true dwelling place.

3. The book of Revelation tells you – in a new way – a story you already know. The apostles tell us that Messiah Jesus died for our sins, that he ascended into the presence of God in heaven, that the message about him is to be proclaimed

throughout the world and that he will return in glory as king and judge. The visions of the book express these things and their consequences.

4. The book does not necessarily go in chronological order. It goes in the order in which I received the visions. At points, it celebrates the end of all things and then goes back to tell the story again from another perspective. It all happens from the point of view of heaven and – you might have guessed it – time works differently there. I suppose that's a good definition of prophecy – to tell people how things are from heaven's perspective.

5. The book is an account of the visions that I received and the fruit of my reflection on those visions. I have written it so that it rewards careful reflection and study. You will see that certain numbers are especially important. We will discuss them as we go.

6. I am not aware of many direct quotations of the Hebrew scriptures in the book. However, it is full of allusions to the Bible. In particular, it would be a good idea to be familiar with the books of Exodus, Psalms, Isaiah, Ezekiel, Daniel and Zechariah. Many of the people in the churches will not know their Bibles well. Part of your job is to help them see how this Revelation fits in with God's previous revelation and forms its climax.

7. The visions tell of things that will happen soon. They've already begun. The task is urgent. The persecution of which Messiah Jesus spoke is already upon us. The book reminds us that the victory over the forces of evil is already won. We now need to remain true to Jesus, persevering in our loyalty to him whatever may be thrown at us – or to whatever we may be thrown!

8. This is a bonus key as we move towards the end of the book. The references to washing and to eating are suggestive of the rituals we practise when we gather. If the church you visit is baptising new believers and/or celebrating the Lord's Supper, these may be great occasions to proclaim the word of God from these visions.

# 1 A fresh perspective

**Revelation 12:1–17**

At this point, the visions went back to the beginning and from my vantage point in heaven I saw things again, this time from what I sensed was a slightly different perspective. I knew how the faithful in Israel had longed for their Messiah. Their suffering had been like the pains of childbirth as they longed for his emergence. Their story is epitomised by one of their number, Mary, the Lord's mother. I watched as a woman strained to deliver her child and saw the struggle of faithful Israel in her wait for her true king. As if things were not bad enough, at this point an enemy appeared, wreaking havoc, determined that the child be destroyed. Your congregations will recognise the way the vision borrows from well-known pagan stories and turns them on their head. The child was snatched away to safety, and, with help from an allusion to Psalm 2, I could see that this was a picture of the death and ascension of Messiah Jesus. He ascended to heaven while his people fled to a place of safety. They find themselves in the wilderness, the place where God shapes his people.

Friends, 1,260 days is 42 months of a nominal 30 days each, which is three and a half years, or times, a time and half a time, as it is put elsewhere. As you know from your study of Daniel, this number is one half of seven, the number of completeness.

The astonishing vision of the war in heaven was another way of understanding Jesus' ascension and its impact. It's an atonement image! The voice from heaven told me all I needed to know. The chief prosecutor – the one who read out the charge sheet in the heavenly tribunal – had been kicked out and could no longer appear. It was just as our friend Paul wrote in his letter to the Romans – there can be no condemnation, for there's no one to bring the charges!

Sadly, this was not the end of the story. The dragon blamed the woman, the faithful people of God, for his defeat and hunted her down. The woman is carried, just as Israel was at the exodus, and, as then, the enemy tried to wash God's people away with the water of chaos, but creation itself protected them. Yet the persecution continued. The true people of God, their inward life, is protected even if their outward form, their bodies, face death.

# 2 The monster emerges

I had been meditating on the prophecy of Daniel and now it seemed to be happening before my eyes. This monster combined features of different beasts in the ancient prophecy, and it represents the spiritual reality that, in our day, lies behind Rome and will lie behind all future powers that do not acknowledge the authority of the true God and that claim his rights as their own. In our time, its heads are the Caesars, who are the earthly manifestations of its power, and the one that seemed to have come back to life, in a mockery of the Lord's resurrection, is Nero, who led the violent persecution experienced by our brothers and sisters in Rome. The death blow is given it by Jesus at the cross in fulfilment of the promise in Genesis (3:15). The spiritual powers, defeated but still active, demand worship; they insist on having everyone's ultimate allegiance. Any rival to this allegiance has to be destroyed. However, God promises to protect the inner life of those who give their loyalty to him.

The monster launched his attack against God's people, for they were alone of all the people of the Roman empire in refusing to be loyal to him. Instead, they had put their trust in the one we call the Lamb, who God planned to offer for us before the world began.

A second monster emerged this time from the earth itself. It acted as a priest, a prophet, a public relations officer for the first beast. It was capable of those distorted miracles, the kind you get in the imperial cult. It deceived the people into believing that the empire and its representatives had ultimate value. Those who refused to acknowledge this, it persecuted. It controlled the markets and the guilds so that any not loyal to it lost their livelihoods.

The first monster has a number. It is a number based on the numeric value of the Hebrew letters that spell the name Nero Caesar. They total 666. If you want to recognise the monster, consider Nero: the megalomania, the arrogance, the brutality and, let's face it, among many, the popularity.

# 3 Salvation and judgement: two visions of Jesus

Each vision is marked by the words 'I looked'. I saw the Lord with his people. The 144,000 we met earlier, who I now knew stood for the universal people of God, were Jesus' army of martyrs. Like the armies of the Hebrew Bible, they were sexually abstinent, and this symbolised their single-minded devotion to following their Lord. They are in the heavenly temple with the living creatures and the elders. They are the first fruits of a greater harvest to come.

An angel appeared, representing the church's faithful proclamation of the gospel to the whole world, while a second and third angel made it clear that the gospel is a double-edged sword that brings salvation to those who are loyal to Jesus but judgement to those who stay loyal to the empire.

The second vision was of Jesus acting in judgement. And I saw an astonishing picture of the impact of God's wrath: the extent of the harvest, the number of grapes gathered and the amount of blood that flowed from them. And then I realised something. The wine press was outside the city, just as the Lord had been when he was crucified. This picture of judgement was of the judgement that fell at Calvary, the wrath that fell on Jesus, and the amount of blood was a picture of the extent of the sacrifice and the unimaginable degree of forgiveness that it could offer. And I realised that I was seeing the extent of the atonement available in Jesus and the full harvest of which the first vision showed the first fruits.

# 4 The beginning of the end

At this point, the visions start moving towards their climax. There will be seven more angels announcing judgement, but these will be the last of them. The angels that I saw here make appearances through the rest of the book.

In a scene with strong echoes of the exodus, I saw the people of God, that is, all those who had stayed faithful to him in the midst of persecution, *standing* beside a sea. The song they sang is very different from the one in Exodus, but I knew that it reflected Moses as well as Jesus. It contained the assurance of the fulfilment of the promise to Abraham, that is celebrated so often in the Psalms and the prophets, that all nations will worship the true God.

Then the shrine within heaven was opened, and there were seven angels whose sashes reminded me of the clothes the priests wore when they officiated in the earthly temple.

They were each given a bowl of the last of God's wrath. I could no longer enter the heavenly Holy of Holies and watched developments from outside.

# 5 The last of God's judgements

Revelation 16

The first four judgements fall first on the earth, then the sea, next the fresh water and finally on the visible heavens. The pattern is close to the one I saw at the blowing of the seven trumpets. However, this time the judgements impact neither a quarter nor a third of their targets, but fall on anything up to the whole of them. The judgements are aimed mainly at the allies of the monster and are in response to their violence towards the people of God. Creation itself is the means of judgement. Sadly, even these actions fail to bring about repentance and change.

This idea is reinforced in the remaining bowls. The fifth is a direct attack on the monster and his followers. The sixth dries up the Euphrates, the symbolic edge of the land, so that there is no barrier to an invasion from the east. The frogs and other details echo the exodus story. The dragon and its monstrous allies are now desperate and send out demonic emissaries to gather allies for one last battle against God. Armageddon is both a reference to the mountain of Megiddo and a kind of portmanteau word combining Gomorrah (Genesis 18:20; 19:24–28) and Nod (Genesis 4:16), both spelled backwards, to indicate a place opposed to the purposes of God and away from his presence. The final bowl is poured into the air and a voice from heaven, in an echo of Jesus' word from the cross, declares that judgement is over. The covenant signs appear for the final time and everywhere there are indications that creation is unravelling – the necessary prelude to its renewal.

However, it is also clear that these events are not fully developed. That development will come in the visions that follow; these will fill out the details.

# 6  Babylon One

It was one of the seven angels with the bowls who led me, so I knew that this was a development of what I had just witnessed. I was told to expect something corrupt that corrupted others. The woman – a parody of the woman I saw earlier who represents the faithful people of God and is carried by him – looked for all the world like the goddess Roma, the spirit of Rome, the mother of its people. She rode upon, was carried by, the monster I'd seen earlier that represented the political power of the empire. The name on her head was Babylon, and I realised that Rome was a manifestation of the same spirit that lay behind that ancient enemy of God's people. Both were drunk on their own power and both were dizzy with their desire to oppress anyone who dared to suggest that ultimate value and purpose lay elsewhere.

The woman was intriguing and seemed to offer great things. This twisted hope would deceive those who did not follow Jesus wholeheartedly. The monster she rode kept trying to mimic God, to stand in his place. And it kept falling short. Where the true God *is*, the monster *is not*.

The vision of the kings, with its sevens and its one to come, simply reinforces the truth that the enemy is a parody of the true God and his Messiah, who has come and is yet to come. The main point is that the moment of hearing is the crucial moment – today is the day of decision. The empire will serve the monster but will be defeated by Jesus the Lamb and his martyr army, and everyone who hears must decide which side to take. The details are less important than the principle – eventually, the empire will turn on Rome; evil will consume itself.

# Guidelines

- The prophet saw things from the vantage point of heaven. If we could see today's world from that perspective, what would we notice?

- What reflections do you have on the idea that many of the visions of Revelation are not about the future but offer perspectives on atonement already accomplished by Jesus?

- Some have argued that Revelation is in part a meditation on Psalm 110:1, a text that may be alluded to at 3:21. Our book tells the story of the process by which, as Messiah Jesus sits at God's right hand, all his enemies are made subject to him. Read through all the places in the New Testament this verse is mentioned (e.g. Matthew 22:41–46; Mark 12:35–37; Luke 20:41–44; Acts 2:34–35; 1 Corinthians 15:25; Hebrews 1:13). Identify the different ways the text is used and then consider whether any of these uses may have helped shape the thinking behind Revelation.

# 1 Babylon Two

The next angel, a remarkable being, announced that Rome, called Babylon, had fallen. These are the two empires that destroyed the temple in Jerusalem. The same spirit that opposes God inspires both of them and will no doubt inspire others in the future. Rome was taunted, using the form of a lament, by the angel's song, and her impending ruin was celebrated as though it has already happened. There are hints in the song, which draws on Isaiah, Jeremiah and Ezekiel, of all the cities who have opposed and rejected God: Babel, Sodom, Nineveh, Tyre and so on.

The kings who depend on Roman power and the merchants who depend on Roman wealth lost everything. They had no scruples, but would trade in whatever could be sold for profit, even in human lives. Small wonder, then, that God's people were told to have nothing to do with the system they represent. And the people of God delighted in hearing the promise of the city's destruction.

All this happened because Rome had killed God's people – but not them alone. The spiritual power behind Rome was responsible for the deaths of *all* those who had ever been slaughtered. This city, this way of organising human life, with its violence and arrogance, must fall so that God's city, God's way of organising human life, can emerge.

# 2 Heavenly voices

Then my attention was drawn once more to the multitude of saints in heaven. The angel had announced the judgement against the empire that held power through oppression, and now the verdict was celebrated. All the attributes claimed by Rome, and other empires like it, belong truly to God alone. And God has rightly judged the empire.

Some people in the congregations you visit may find the language used distasteful. Remind them that the poetry is intended to generate revulsion and that throughout the scriptures sexual misconduct functions as a meta-phor for spiritual failings. God's judgement falls because of idolatry. That is to say that the empires of the world gave themselves ultimate value and saw themselves as the source of salvation, authority and glory. The outcome of this was that they martyred all those who found true value anywhere else, including, most especially, the people who worshipped the true God. It is not so much that the martyrs will be avenged as that they will be vindicated – they will be shown to have been in the right.

The culmination of all things is depicted as a marriage feast and the groom is to be the King Jesus. If sexual immorality stands for idolatry, this marriage is an expression of true worship.

# 3  A second white horse

**Revelation 19:11–21**

I was still outside the heavenly Holy of Holies, and as I watched another white horse emerged. This time there is no doubt about the rider. This is the prom-ised bridegroom, and his appearance is shaped by the great wedding song we know as Psalm 45. The rider had a secret name so that none could say he was fully known to them and none could claim to control him. Even before the battle, his robe was red with blood. The blood was his own, shed for the sins of the world. He was followed by his martyr army. His only weapon was what came from his mouth – his word – but with this the whole world was conquered. This is the fulfilment of the words of Psalm 2. These are words that promise judgement, but always remember that judgement fell at Calvary.

Then, like Ezekiel, I witnessed the carrion-eating birds that occupy the visible heavens being summoned to the scene between the monster and the kings who followed him and Messiah Jesus and his martyrs. The monster and his chief ally were utterly destroyed. Their allies died through the word of the Messiah, and the carrion-eaters, in a parody of the king's wedding supper, swooped to feast. The word of Jesus was victorious. The spiritual realities behind the world's empires were destroyed forever. As for the humans who had allied themselves to those empires, their flesh, their outward being, was consumed. Their opposition was over. But their inner beings continued, for they had yet to face the final judgement and the decisive second death.

# 4 The fate of the enemy

The pattern of the vision broadly follows the one you know from Ezekiel. But I realised this was another atonement vision – I was seeing the impact of the cross. The abyss was the place from which evil emerged, and it is to there that the enemy was confined for a thousand years. All the names the scriptures give to the figures who distort the word of God are ascribed to this enemy. He is the spirit behind the one who deceived Adam and Eve, the one who tried to draw King Jesus away from his true calling and the one who reminded God of the wrongdoings of his people.

More than this, in every land but Israel, his distorted version of the truth had held sway. Only in Israel was the true God acknowledged; the rest of the world was deceived. But now, because of the atoning work of Jesus, the scales would fall from the eyes of the nations. The promise made to Abraham – that through his descendants, all the nations would be blessed – was about to be fulfilled. The words of the psalms summoning all the nations to worship would finally get a response. For a thousand years, a symbol for an age that would last for as long as the purposes of God required, the nations would be deceived no longer and would turn, in faith, to the true God. As the King said, the gospel must be preached to all nations.

The souls of the martyrs reigned with Jesus through this period, though their bodies were not yet restored to them and this was the first phase of their resurrection. This was God's answer to the prayer they uttered when the fifth seal was opened.

At the end of the gospel age, the enemy rallied one last time but was utterly destroyed by heaven. The universe was prepared for the final judgement and there was no place for anyone to hide. All were now embodied, resurrected to face judgement. All were judged in accordance with their deeds, but the names of some were found in the scroll of life and these were spared the fate of the enemy. It is the King's book, the outcome of his atoning work, that has the final word in the judgement. Death and Hades, spiritual realities that hold humans in thrall, are destroyed forever; their power is broken once and for all. The second death is final and those who face it are lost. It is the destruction of the inner being as well as the body. There is no appeal.

# 5 Cosmic renewal

I saw the new heavens, and the sea, that ancient source of chaos, was no more. This renewal would be definitive. Heaven had known the presence of the enemy and was now to be transformed; it even, as I saw in my vision of the Holy of Holies, had contained a sea of a kind (4:6), a constant and restless potential source of disorder. The sea was now gone. The great city of oppression and violence had definitively fallen, and the holy city emerged. This city is the King's bride. It descended to earth so the two could meet, and I remembered the story of Babel (Genesis 11:1–9) and saw that where the human project to build a tower to the heavens had failed dismally, God had, through the atoning work of his Son, brought heaven down to us. The last great division, that between God and humans, heaven and earth, was overcome and the creation was healed. God's dwelling, his tent, his tabernacle, was now among humans, completing the tabernacling spoken of in the gospel. You remember the feast of tabernacles with its great themes of water and light? Well, watch out for them in the vision of the renewed creation!

Astonishingly, I saw that the one people of God was made up of many peoples, that the renewed creation retained echoes of human differences now transformed into a picture of perfect unity in diversity. Once again, there is an echo of a word from the cross: it is done! The section finishes with a promise that echoes those made in the seven letters. There are many such links between the letters and the closing visions of the book. Point them out to the churches and help them to see the connection between who they are now and what they have been promised, and compare this with the fate of those whose deeds mean that the second death awaits.

Then I realised that this vision was all part of the preceding ones, for the angel that announced things had poured out one of the seven bowls; judgement and salvation are two sides of the same coin. The King's bride was a city with gates. It had the shape of a giant cube, the same shape as the Holy of Holies in the temple, and I realised that this was the heavenly Holy of Holies where I had seen the throne of God now being joined to the earth. The city was dressed in the jewels belonging to the breastplate of the high priest. The culmination of the great work of atonement was being presented – God and humans would be one. And I understood that if humans had never disobeyed God, they would not have remained in the garden but that, under their stewardship, the earth would have journeyed to a moment like this. But the humans who had that joy would not have known the deeper joy of those who understand the depths of love shown by the God who saw the task to completion at the most astonishing cost to himself. There was no temple in the city because, in one sense, it was all temple; it is the place where God tabernacles.

Astonishingly, I saw that the nations remained, in an image inspired by Isaiah, walking by the light of this city. As in Zechariah's picture, there was no night. I saw that there were kings who were bringing the best they had to the city in homage. Once they had brought the very best they had to the city called Babylon, but now it was brought to the city of God. Its gates were open so that people could go in and out, but there was no room there for idolatry or deceit. Remind the congregations that there is no place among God's people for such things.

# 6 The final scene

**Revelation 22**

The same angel continued my tour, and it was like a combination of the story of Eden from Genesis and the promised temple from Ezekiel. Humans are where God always intended that we should end up – in this great city that is God's dwelling place. Remember the story in Genesis where the cherubim were posted to guard the way to the tree of life? All that is now overturned, and the trees offer a harvest every month. The process that will lead to this point is already underway. If you hold to these promises, you will know God's blessing and you will accomplish what the psalmist longed for – you will see the face of God. You will bear God's own name on your forehead, just like the high priests of the earthly temple. Remember the priestly blessing, 'The Lord make his face to shine upon you'? That will be your experience.

Make sure you hammer home the reliability of these words and the urgency of the right response. In the end, this can be summed up as worshipping the true God and so avoiding any form of idolatry.

Unlike Daniel's great work, my prophecy is unsealed – you are to take it out and proclaim God's word in it and from it.

Remember that from first to last, it's all about Jesus; he's first, he's last, he's everything! There can be no half measures; you're either forgiven, baptised and following, or you're an outsider. Jesus is the first sign that God's eternal day is on its way – he's the star that heralds the dawn. And we long for him; the Spirit within the church longs for his coming, just as Jesus still bids us to come to him.

Now, as you go out to share these prophecies with the churches and interpret them, you may find yourself tempted to add supplements of your own or perhaps to leave out parts of them. That would mislead the churches and you would face serious consequences.

The book ends with a promise, a prayer and a blessing: the promise of Jesus that he will soon come, the prayer of the church that he should do so and a blessing on us while we wait for the event that fulfils the promise and answers the prayer.

The book began as a letter and it ends as a letter. The words 'testify', 'soon' and 'grace' and the themes addressed tie these concluding sentences to the greetings at the start of the letter. We have come full circle. What you have heard you must now proclaim. And what you must read and proclaim you must summon the churches to live out.

## Guidelines

- The city's gates are open, the wicked have been condemned to the lake of fire and yet there appear to be some who still exist and yet are outside the city. How would you sum up the tension between the text's universalist vision, its consignment of the wicked to the lake of fire and the continuing presence of those described in 22:15 as being 'outside'?

- Revelation insists that judgement is by works. Yet elsewhere it speaks of the water of life being a gift and of those who wash their robes. How does the book hold these tensions together?

- The book ends with a warning for those who add or take away from the words of the prophecy. Has the church you are part of done either of these things? Have we heeded the warning?

- Think about the relationship between Revelation and the sacraments of the church. The text often speaks of washing, which may well speak of baptism. In addition, ancient liturgies link the expression 'Come, Lord Jesus' to the celebration of the Lord's Supper, which Paul tells us we will do 'until he comes'.

**FURTHER READING**

Richard Bauckham, *The Theology of the Book of Revelation* (CUP, 1993).

Gregory K. Beale, *The Book of Revelation: A commentary on the Greek text* (Eerdmans, 1999).

Allan Boesak, *Comfort and Protest: Reflections on the apocalypse of John of Patmos* (Wipf and Stock, 2001).

Wes Howard-Brook and Anthony Gwyther, *Unveiling Empire: Reading Revelation then and now* (Orbis, 1999).

John Sweet, *Revelation* (SCM, 1990).

# Advent and Christmas visitors

## David Spriggs

Entertaining family and friends is an essential part of celebrating Christmas. It is often a great joy to be able to get together and relax over food and drinks. It's an opportunity to catch up on the months since last we met and to share some of our hopes for the future. Sometimes these occasions are mixed with an element of obligation. We feel we need to invite certain members of the family, because they are family, but anticipate their presence will generate challenges for the rest. But it's Christmas, the season of good will! Many of us also welcome lonely neighbours or elderly friends who might otherwise be on their own.

Lots of churches go a step further, organising meals or even shelter for the homeless or putting on Christmas lunches for the lonely.

In many ways this is simply how human relationships work. But it is also 'gospel territory'. The Advent and Christmas stories are full of visitors, some family, some strangers, but all bringing some relevant message for this season. We will explore these together over the next week, not forgetting, of course, the essential, primary visitor, who came to his own people, but they did not want to know.

It is also worth reflecting on the fact that every time we read or engage with scripture, we are visitors. We enter another home, another culture, another time. So, as with visiting, we remember we need to be respectful of the text, for it belongs to someone else and we are guests. We remember, too, that we will leave it soon, and how we leave it will impact those who follow. But hopefully we will have treasured memories and stories to share of the time we spent there. We will have been transformed, maybe a little, maybe a lot.

Bible quotations are taken from the NIV.

# 1 An angel and Zechariah: who is the visitor?

**Luke 1:5–22**

Luke begins his gospel with a story of a divine visitation – that of the angel to Zechariah. Our week's reflections will end with the ultimate divine visitation, the birth of Jesus, while Luke's gospel will end with this visitor leaving the disciples – but with the promise of much more to come (see Luke 24:49–53).

To describe our reading as a 'divine visitation' is only half the story and might even be misleading. For Zechariah, now an old man, is a visitor too. He is a faithful and upright priest who carries a deep disappointment which he shares with his equally pious wife, Elizabeth. Their disappointment is that they have no child to continue the line of priesthood and they are beyond childbearing age. This hope has gone forever. Zechariah is a visitor because his section of the priesthood has gone to Jerusalem to serve in the temple. He has visited Jerusalem many times before. Now he has the opportunity to go further, probably further than he has ever been before – he will visit the Holy Place to burn incense on behalf of all the people. This was a privilege that many priests would only get once in a lifetime, if at all. It was like not only visiting Buckingham Palace, but also being selected from the crowd to go in and meet the Queen! Zechariah was the visitor in the sacred place of the Most High. The angel, as God's messenger and visible presence, had more right to be there than he did. Indeed, the text says, the angel 'appeared' not 'he arrived' (v. 11).

Zechariah 'was startled and was gripped with fear' (v. 12) and with good reason. He had just seen an angel, 'at the right side of the altar'. Perhaps his mind flashed back to the book that bore his name. There an angel has 'Satan standing at the right side to accuse him' (Zechariah 3:1; see also Job 2:1). Was Zechariah about to be accused? Did Zechariah carry the nagging doubt that he was childless and heirless because of some secret sin? Was this to be revealed?

As we approach Christmas, we remember that visiting sacred places and special times can be disturbing, even if we think we are hosting others.

# 2 An angel visits Mary: a vulnerable young woman

Luke 1:26–38

This must be one of the best-known and most life-changing visits ever recorded, not only within the Bible but also in human history. Please note the language. 'God *sent* the angel Gabriel *to* Nazareth… *to* a virgin' (v. 26, my italics). Here we are left in no doubt: the angel Gabriel is the visitor and Mary the host. Rather unusually, this does not put her in the position of power and control!

It is often the case that the visitor is disadvantaged with respect to the host. The host can either welcome or reject the visitor. They can make them feel welcome or uncomfortable. They can give the visitor the run of the house or carefully proscribe their freedoms. But this angel is in full control. The story is full of the angel's clear and complete message. Once the message is delivered, 'the angel left her' (v. 38). Mary only appears in three short places in the text (vv. 29, 34, 38). These, especially the latter two, are however crucial interventions. Mary has no say as to whether the angel meets her (there is no indication she was at home, so she had no control about letting her visitor in to her life), nor about whether she will let him speak. Mary is not only a virgin, but she is also vulnerable.

Perhaps we can become more sensitive to our own 'positions of power', even when we are visiting others, whether in person, on the phone or by text or social media, and even within our own homes and among our families. This angel seeks to reassure Mary at every possible opportunity (for example, assuring her there was nothing to fear, affirming her by saying she was favoured by God twice, giving her positive news and letting her know he understood her personally by using her name and relating to Elizabeth's situation).

But back to those two interventions. First, Mary is allowed to ask for clarification (v. 34). When we are the visitor or in some other way in the position of power, it is good to allow others to clarify with us what we mean or to share their concerns or their anxieties. The angel clearly listened and equally clearly clarified Mary's concerns and reassured her. Second, Mary was allowed to offer and articulate her own response (v. 38).

# 3 Mary's visit to Elizabeth: welcoming an unexpected guest

**Luke 1:39–56**

These days with mobile phones we can arrange to meet with great precision and alert the person to our arrival. Yet the ancient world also had its effective means of communication. Whether Elizabeth was expecting Mary to visit her, we will never know.

What we are told is that Mary left Nazareth for the 'hill country of Judea', an imprecise geographical reference, 'at that time' also being an imprecise temporal reference, but did so in a hurry. This word can mean 'very quickly', 'on the spur of the moment' or with 'eagerness' and 'enthusiasm'. What Luke conveys to us is that having absorbed the angel's news of an unlikely but impending pregnancy, Mary heads for her much older relative. We can speculate whether she did that to avoid the embarrassment and indeed danger of being spotted as pregnant out of wedlock (see Deuteronomy 22:20–21) or because she needed someone to talk to and support her, or because she had heard about Elizabeth's equally surprising pregnancy. Again we'll never know.

What we do know is that on arrival Mary received a special welcome. Of course, it was an important part of their culture to welcome people with attentiveness and feasting (see for example Genesis 18:1–8; Luke 7:44–46), but Elizabeth's welcome is in another class! But the person she actually welcomes is not only Mary but the recently conceived baby in her womb: 'Blessed are you among women, and blessed is the child you will bear!' (v. 42).

Luke presents this greeting as 'charismatic' and probably prophetic. As soon as Elizabeth hears Mary's voice, 'the baby leaped in her womb, and Elizabeth was filled with the Holy Spirit. In a loud voice she exclaimed…' (vv. 41–42).

In all probability, Luke intends us to understand that the recognition that Mary was pregnant, as well as the nature of the conception and the stature of the baby (see verse 43, 'my Lord'), are a divine revelation through the Holy Spirit. Manifestations of the Holy Spirit will be a significant part of Luke's two-part narrative. The note of joy, divinely given insights and words of prophecy will be critical. So, early on, he emphasises that it is Jesus who triggers these. And noteworthy, too, that it is a woman who leads the way.

Thus, Elizabeth welcomes not only Mary but the even more unexpected guest in Mary's womb with a threefold blessing. But then, she was of priestly lineage (1:5)!

# 4  Joseph and Mary visit Bethlehem: where do they stay?

Luke 2:1–7; 22:7–12

Many people's picture of the first Christmas is something like this: Mary (on a donkey) and Joseph arrive in Bethlehem as darkness falls and the winter cold intensifies. They visit several inns and are told everywhere is full. Eventually (perhaps reluctantly) a kindly innkeeper allows them to use his stable. So when the shepherds (and Magi too?) arrive, Jesus is in the manger, the stable is full of animals (and birds) and the proud parents look on.

The biblical account bears little resemblance to this. There is no donkey mentioned, and there is no statement that they went from inn to inn searching for a room. There seems to be no mention of a stable either!

Let's deal with the stable first. It seems a reasonable deduction because of the mention of 'the manger', but in peasant homes the mangers could be built of stone and positioned between the living quarters and the lower part where the animals were kept overnight. However, that is not quite the whole story. Three times 'the manger' is referred to (2:7, 12, 16). This word can also mean 'stall' or 'stable', as at 13:15). Presumably translators prefer 'manger' in Luke 2, as it is difficult to see how you would 'lay' a baby in a stable. But we need to be aware that our conceptual reconstruction is probably rather different to the reality!

The same probably applies to 'inn'. It is worth noting that the word so translated is not the normal word for a commercial inn. Luke's word for 'inn' here is also used by him for the guest room where the Passover will be commemorated. This is further defined as a 'large room upstairs' (see 22:11–12). The guest room was either on the roof or an extension on the back of the single-family room. It was this guest room which was full; a very inappropriate place to give birth.

Mary and Joseph were given the best hospitality and the maximum privacy the owner (probably a relative) could provide in the circumstances. This was either in the lower part of the house where the animals were kept overnight or even at that end of the single-family room with the feeding trough between them.

# 5  Angels and shepherds: why bother visiting?

Luke 2:8–20

Why do people bother visiting? Often it's to catch up with friends. Sometimes it is more to do with curiosity – we want to know what a place or building, or even a picture, actually looks like. Why do large crowds of people attend football matches when they could watch it at home, without the journey and the parking costs? Why did the shepherds go to Bethlehem and risk both the safety of their sheep and their livelihoods? There is no report that the angel told them to go! Fortunately we are told their reason: 'Let's go to Bethlehem and *see* this thing that has happened, which the Lord has told us about' (v. 15, my italics).

So it was to 'see' it. Was it to check that it was true? Was it that they didn't want to miss the party?

We can find out about other countries and cities through TV programmes, which give us more insight than we would possibly get ourselves. We can take 360-degree virtual tours of important buildings, providing us with details we would miss on our own. The recent Covid-19 pandemic has raised in a more acute form the question of whether we need to visit. We can talk to relatives by FaceTime and meet on Zoom. But somehow, none of these is as good as seeing for ourselves. Indeed, most people have become more convinced than ever that there is no substitute for being there in person.

Perhaps there are two main components as to why this is the case. The shepherds spoke of 'seeing' what had happened. But it wasn't just visual! When we are there, we absorb the scene or event with a whole symphony of senses. For many of us, sight is the primary sense, but it is enhanced by sound, smell, taste and touch, which add context and counterpoint to the visual. And because we are there, we can exercise a freedom to explore the scene for ourselves, to linger on something that fascinates us, however trivial that may be. So our experience is unique. No matter how many different camera angles and video replays we can see, being there is special to us.

The second reason is that it is a shared experience. While you may see more details and close-ups when you watch sport on the TV, when you are part of the crowd, you become part of the story, as the shepherds became – that makes it different.

# 6 Jesus visits our world: a world of difference

John 1:10–18

So now to the heart of it! All the visits of angels, of women, of the holy family, of shepherds and of Magi, focus on this: 'She gave birth to her firstborn, a son' (Luke 2:7).

Yet what is it all about? What does it mean? The angels give some clues to the shepherds, and the Magi have discerned some of it too, but it is John's gospel which takes us to the heart of the matter: 'The Word became flesh and made his dwelling among us' (v. 14).

However, this raises an interesting question for us. Was 'the Word' a visitor? The verb 'dwelling' may suggest to us that he was more than a visitor. But the Greek is less clear. Literally it means to 'tent' among us – which may suggest that it was a short-term visit. However, tents were (and still can be) the lifetime home of the Bedouin. Some commentators link this word to the 'tabernacle' and refer to Exodus 25 and 33:7–11. They may even further deduce that it means 'to take residence'. Others point out that it sounds like the Hebrew for 'to dwell'. Perhaps the best answer is that the Word was a long-term visitor.

However, another point John makes gives us pause to question this description. For we are told that 'he came to that which was his own' (v. 11). Whether 'his own' means Israel or the world, it remains questionable that if you come to something you own you can be described as a visitor. However, you can own something, say a property that you have bought, without actually seeing it in person. Then you could properly be described as visiting it!

What really matters is that the Word's coming is a specific historical happening, which also had limits (i.e. a visit). He would not be among us for-ever. Perhaps of even more significance is the difference this visitor has made:

1 To all who welcome him, he gave the right to become children of God.
2 His coming means that his 'glory' has been seen and can be proclaimed.
3 We have received one blessing after another.
4 He has made known to us the full reality of God as Father.

# Guidelines

Reflecting on some of the 'visitations' associated with Advent and Christmas highlights a number of issues for us to consider more deeply. We select just two.

- *The relationship between visitors and hosts* is complex. Initially it seems that the host is the person in charge, but this is not always the case. There are hidden and unexpressed norms of behaviour which shape the situations. The host is obliged to meet the needs of the visitor and to give them preference; if the visitor takes this as their right, matters can become awkward. The host might expect that the visitor will recognise they are in someone else's home and treat it and also the host with respect. These norms are modulated by the relationship between visitor and host. So when an adult child returns home, they can easily assume it's their home now, just as it used to be before they left. The host might expect that they will help out with the tasks just as they used to, but a sensitive son or daughter returning might feel insecure doing this. Reflect on the power issues between host and visitor in your experiences; seek discernment if during visits (where you are host or visitor) you sense any 'atmosphere'. Pray for any visits, that God's peace will be experienced by all.

- As *churches welcome many visitors* to their Christmas services and activities, it is good to recognise that they have, like the shepherds, come to see for themselves. How can we enhance this experience for them, recognising that seeing means we use all our senses and each of them can become part of the story?

---

**FURTHER READING**

Kenneth E. Bailey, *Jesus through Middle Eastern Eyes: Cultural studies in the gospels* (SPCK, 2008), especially pages 25–37.
I. Howard Marshall, *The Gospel of Luke* (Paternoster 1978).
Tom Wright, *Luke for Everyone* (SPCK, 2001)

# Advent: voices of hope

Jenny Hellyer

As Christians, we are living today in the time between the Incarnation 2,000 years ago and the promised return of Jesus Christ, when he will usher in 'a new heaven and a new earth', where God 'will wipe every tear' (Revelation 21:1, 4).

As we approach Christmas, the season of gifts, we remember with gratitude the gift of the prophets, who saw, by the power of the Spirit, the coming of the Messiah and a future day of peace under his reign.

Jesus has taught us of the hope we have in the age to come, but also to be people of hope in the present.

These readings are an opportunity to hear again some voices of hope and perhaps to grow in, and to grasp afresh, this gift of hope, which God offers to his people to sustain them on their earthly pilgrimage.

Bible quotations are taken from the NIV.

20–26 December

## 1 A child

### Isaiah 9:1–7

Isaiah was writing in the stormy days of an expanding Assyrian empire and the ensuing decline of Israel. There is judgement over nations, but also words of comfort, grace and hope – and finally of God's ultimate purpose, a messianic age, where there will be 'new heavens and a new earth' (Isaiah 65:17).

The prophet speaks for God, who is light (v. 2). Dawn is coming! Perhaps we are reminded here of the shepherds on those dark hills, confronted by angels bathed in light (Luke 2). And today we still declare the coming Saviour's birth in a dark world of sorrow and lovelessness; but where the light of Jesus dawns, a new kingdom grows. Wars cease and joy replaces fear (vv. 3–5).

Who is at the heart of the means of deliverance for us? A little child (v. 6). God overcomes his enemies, not by oppression and coercion, but by becoming vulnerable and humble – the only hope for turning enmity into friendship.

Verses 6–7 are a birth announcement. Furthermore, Isaiah announces the baby's identity and destiny. The 'Wonderful Counsellor' is a king who acts with great wisdom. He is the 'Mighty God', holding the power to conquer. As 'Everlasting Father' he will be the enduring and compassionate protector and provider. His rule as 'Prince of Peace' brings wholeness to individuals and to society.

I wrote this as the terrible coronavirus pandemic spread through the nations. It felt as if we were a people walking in darkness, living in the land of the shadow of death (v. 2). In the midst of loss, lockdown, anxiety and uncertainty, however, the light of Christ was shining – in the selfless risks taken by doctors and nurses and in the kindness shown among communities, sharing resources and care. The church of God online was reaching into lives in great need of light and peace. Priorities became clear. What suffering patients most frequently talked about from their hospital experiences was the sense of being loved. Like Florence Nightingale, the 'lady of the lamp', many were carrying the light of Christ into the darkness, expressed in loving care.

We often speak of light as a symbol of hope – 'light at the end of the tunnel', for example. God brings hope, as light, to us, especially through his Son. As you read again of his qualities in verse 6, notice which touches your mind or heart in some way. Stay with the word or phrase, allowing its meaning to apply to you or a situation. Receive this as a gift as you pray.

# 2  Peace

**Micah 5:2–5**

A contemporary of Isaiah, Micah lived in a village in southern Judah. His message, like Isaiah's, alternates between oracles of doom and oracles of hope, between judgement and deliverance. He sees the social ills, injustices and empty ritualism which will incur destruction: 'a siege is laid against us' (v. 1).

Verse 2 starts with that word of hope: 'But'! How often in scripture, and in our lives, God's compassion breaks in (see 7:19). In the passage we read of the promise of a wonderful ruler, to be born from a small clan in an insignificant location. Mysteriously, Micah asserts that his origins are 'from of old', pointing perhaps to an eternal reality.

As we read on, it is clear that such a ruler is from God himself, possessing a shepherd heart and the strength and majesty of the Lord. Jesus, the fulfilment of this hope, often spoke of his unity with God the Father, possessing just these qualities. The prophecy is of a kingdom extending across the whole world, thus ensuring security. A beautiful image of human flourishing occurs in the previous chapter: 'Everyone will sit under their own vine and under their own fig-tree, and no one will make them afraid, for the Lord Almighty has spoken' (4:4).

'He will be our peace' (5:5). The Messiah not only ends war in the world, but also war within each of us. 'Who is a God like you, who pardons sin and forgives the transgression…? You do not stay angry forever but delight to show mercy' (7:18). The promise of forgiveness and mercy was pledged long ago to Abraham (7:20) and is still held out to God's broken world today: 'But as for me, I watch in hope for the Lord, I wait for God my Saviour; my God will hear me' (7:7).

Knowing that God hears you, bring to him what is on your heart or in your concerns today. He delights to show you mercy, so rest in his peace, receiving all that he wants to give you to sustain you. The peace of the Lord be with you.

# 3  Light

**Luke 1:57–79**

Prophecy not only predicts but also proclaims. Here God declares, through the voice of Zechariah, the imminent fulfilment of these ancient prophetic promises (compare verse 69 with Jeremiah 23:5; verse 72 with Micah 7:20; and verse 78 with Malachi 4:2).

In this passage there is a wonderful collision between the homeliness of a birth, celebrated by kindly neighbours and relatives (provoking an argument about appropriate names), and the sudden return of speech to Zechariah, where it feels as if heaven itself breaks in at the moment he insists on God's choice of name: 'To everyone's astonishment he wrote, "His name is John." Immediately his mouth was opened and his tongue set free, and he began to speak, praising God' (v. 63–64). Zechariah's earlier voice of cynicism (1:18), debating with the angel, is transformed into a voice of hope. Those neighbours are now filled with awe (v. 65).

Zechariah speaks words and truths that could only have been given him by the Holy Spirit. The dramatic power of the words is somehow reminiscent of the opening of Genesis, as God spoke each element of life into existence ('"Let there be light," and there was light', Genesis 1:3). And now, for the redemption of this creation, his voice is again speaking of salvation, forgiveness and peace.

Light, for us, is a wonderful symbol of hope and life: the 'rising sun' (v. 78) echoes Isaiah 9:2 ('a light has dawned'). God intends good: he sees those 'walking in darkness' and 'in the land of deep darkness' and prepares a new day for his beloved world. He sends Zechariah's son, John, to prepare us all for his Son, Jesus.

Twice in this passage we read of mercy (vv. 72, 78). When heaven breaks in, it is 'because of the tender mercy of our God'. Mercy can be described as the love that responds to human need in an unexpected or unmerited way. At its core is a posture of forgiveness. It is costly compassion. The promised Saviour, 'being in very nature God, did not consider equality with God something to be used to his own advantage; rather, he made himself nothing... He humbled himself by becoming obedient to death – even death on a cross!' (Philippians 2:6–8). This was the cost of God's mercy.

Using the image of light, bring to God situations or people you see 'walking in darkness' – be it in pain, hardship or a life without hope – and ask for the light of our tender-hearted God to shine on them.

# 4  Trust

**Lamentations 3:19–26**

The prophet Jeremiah is traditionally considered to be the author of Lamentations, a series of five laments expressing the huge sense of loss that accompanied Jerusalem's destruction – including its temple – and the exile of many to Babylon in 586BC. He had previously prophesied extensively concerning Judah's sin, suffering much hostility as he spoke of God's impending judgement.

Despite his personal pain, and that of Judah, Jeremiah has not lost sight of God's covenant love. This passage, at the heart of the book, is a profound testimony of trust in the God of love (v. 22), hope (v. 21, 24–25), faithfulness (v. 23) and salvation (v. 26); these are verses to meditate on, in times of both personal and national sorrow or conflict, for Jeremiah reminds us that the Lord is good and will act in our lives with loving 'compassions' (v. 22) – they are 'new every morning' (v. 23). Day by day, God accompanies us with his provisions of grace.

There is a sense that Jeremiah, over time, has had to teach himself to inhabit these truths. He remembers his afflictions (v. 19), yet he 'calls to mind' what is needed to live from hope (v. 21). As he reflects on this faithful God, he 'says to himself' that the Lord is all he needs (v. 24), so therefore he will wait in hope. Suffering has tested Jeremiah, and yet it has refined his faith and his discipline. This is an encouragement for us in dark times, to call to mind God's faithfulness and to take ourselves in hand.

Paul, writing to the Corinthian Christians, expresses the same hope, refined by extensive trials:

*Therefore we do not lose heart… For our light and momentary troubles are achieving for us an eternal glory that far outweighs them all. So we fix our eyes not on what is seen, but on what is unseen, since what is seen is temporary, but what is unseen is eternal.*

2 CORINTHIANS 4:16–18

*The Lord is good to those whose hope is in him, to the one who seeks him; it is good to wait quietly for the salvation of the Lord.*

LAMENTATIONS 3:25–26

As a way of following Jeremiah on his journey of trust:

1  Read the passage slowly two or three times, aloud if possible. Notice a word or phrase that seems to strike you as you read.
2  Stay with this word or words and reflect quietly on them. Let them lead your thoughts.
3  Turn some of your reflections into prayer, simply speaking to God.

The Lord is good to those whose hope is in him.

# 5  Christ in you

## Colossians 1:1–13

We have heard from the prophetic voices – of Isaiah, Micah, Jeremiah and Zechariah (father of John the Baptist) – declaring a future hope, in both a Messiah and one day a new heaven and earth. Here, from a prison in Rome, the apostle Paul affirms that God has now sent Jesus, the long-promised light, to rescue us from 'the dominion of darkness' (v. 13) and bring us into 'the kingdom of light' (v. 12) with him.

Paul's letter refutes a heresy in Colossae, with its accompanying attitudes and practices, which drew people away from the complete centrality and adequacy of Jesus, around 60 years after his birth, death and resurrection.

He commends the Christians for their faith and love, which 'spring from the hope stored up for you in heaven' (v. 5). Hope here is not wishful thinking, but the assured gift from a loving God to his children 'held out' (offered) in the gospel (v. 23). Notice how Paul emphasises the truth of the gospel (vv. 5–6); he wants the believers to be confident in their faith in Jesus.

This passage describes beautifully what it is to live in the context of eternal hope. This life is all by God's grace, a gifting through the power of the Spirit of Christ in us – whether in wisdom (v. 9), fruitfulness (v. 10), strength to endure (v. 11) or gratitude (v. 12).

Thérèse of Lisieux wrote often about living a life of grace. Here she is speaking of her task as a novice mistress for young nuns:

*The knowledge that it was impossible to do anything of myself greatly simplified my task… The one aim of my interior life was to unite myself more and more closely with God. My hope has never been deceived. Each time I needed food for the souls in my charge, I always found my hands filled. Had I acted otherwise, and relied on my own strength, I should very soon have been forced to give up.*

From *The Story of a Soul*, chapter 11

God fills us (v. 9) and strengthens us (v. 11) for a fruitful life.

Thérèse beautifully expresses the faith and love which Paul sees in the Colossians (v. 4–5); she humbly offers us the secret of bearing fruit (v. 10), which is to be happily dependent on the Spirit, Christ within. And we discern her joy (v. 12).

At the heart of Paul's encouragement is a message of grace. Hope is stored up for us. We are, by his Spirit, gifted in every way to be people of hope, faith and love. A response might be both thanksgiving and a prayer to be filled anew with his Spirit – to continue to be dependent on him for everything.

'Christ in you, the hope of glory' (Colossians 1:27).

# 6 Grace

Christian hope is not vague wishful thinking, but a wonderful and sustaining gift of grace from the God who has loved his creation from before time began. The coming of Jesus Christ, and his sacrificial death 'at just the right time' (v. 6), demonstrated this love for a fallen world. Hope, then, is founded on eternal love, expressed supremely in the incarnation and resurrection 2,000 years ago.

In our day-to-day living, Paul encourages us to 'boast in the hope of the glory of God' (v. 2), our future destiny; we shall be as he is, because of grace. We see glimpses of this glory in one another as God's grace transforms us.

After speaking of glory, Paul speaks of 'sufferings' (v. 3). How can we 'glory in our sufferings'? They are not meaningless from an eternal perspective, but contain redemption: the fruits of perseverance, character and hope (v. 4). This hope is not blind optimism, but the assurance that has been stimulated and refined in the fire of our human trials.

Perseverance is the mark of the Christian holding on to the grace of a loving Father whose purposes they trust. The writer to the Hebrews also encourages us to 'hold firmly to our confidence and the hope in which we glory' (Hebrews 3:6). It is worth noticing that Paul is writing to the Christian community in Rome, not to an individual; we can uphold one another in the seasons of suffering through prayer and companionship, and we can encourage each other through words of grace and hope. Jesus, by his Spirit, accompanies us all (v. 10).

Above all, believers learn to rejoice in God himself (v. 11). The hope of glory is a joyful hope; finding God's presence and purposes in the midst of suffering is a cause for joy. But no joy is comparable to that found in God himself. Paul has just outlined the outrageous grace of God's love (vv. 6–10), which restores friendship with him and utterly transforms life. We are loved! We become hope-bearers.

Give thanks for the hope of glory Jesus has won for us because of his love. Give thanks that God's presence and purposes accompany us in our suffering. Receive this blessing as a grace from God today:

*May the God of hope fill you with all joy and peace as you trust in him, so that you may overflow with hope by the power of the Holy Spirit.*

ROMANS 15:13

# Guidelines

'Put your hope in God': the psalmist speaks to his 'downcast' soul (Psalm 42:5). 'For I will yet praise him, my Saviour and my God.'

Herein lies the key to our growth as hope-filled people. The psalmist is committed to an openness to, and a trust in, God, even in the midst of great difficulties. 'By day the Lord directs his love, at night his song is with me – a prayer to the God of my life' (v. 8).

How has such conviction and intimacy come about? Nothing can be a substitute for our own resolve to keep trusting and praying, and living in the light of God's love and promises. The psalmist found his 'joy and delight' (Psalm 43:4) not in success and favourable circumstances, but in the one who satisfies our hearts for eternity. We all live with unfulfilled desires in this life, but as we practise putting our hope in the God whose loving purposes will be fully accomplished in the age to come, we will surely become hope-bearers for each other.

'As for me, I watch in hope for the Lord, I wait for God my Saviour' (Micah 7:7).

---

**FURTHER READING**

Walter Brueggemann, *The Prophetic Imagination*, 40th anniversary edition (Fortress Press, 2018).

Tom Wright, *Surprised by Hope* (SPCK, 2007).

# Malachi

## Hazel Sherman

Around four-and-a-half to five centuries before the time of Christ, after an extended period of exile and abandonment, a new temple was built in Jerusalem. The rebuilding of identity (albeit as a province of Persia not a nation state) and a reformation of religious practice and ritual were the twin features of this restoration. It featured prophets, such as Haggai and Zechariah, and leaders, such as Ezra and Nehemiah, who were committed to structuring a national life centred on covenant with God and purity in relationship. We don't know how far this reached out into the scattered groups and communities away from the centre in Jerusalem, but it is a significant stage in the biblical witness: testimony to the theme of exile and restoration which is never 'done and dusted' so long as there are people around to mess things up for themselves and others.

We have no biographical or personal information about Malachi, whose name is the same as the book's title, 'My Messenger'. We do know that in his time, while the temple is rebuilt and open for business, God has a continuing controversy with those who organise and take part in its worship: their lives are not matching up to what God has commanded. This controversy is conducted through a series of argumentative exchanges in which God and the people accuse one another of neglect. Through the progression of the book, the moral weakness of the people's complaint is countered by the weighty concerns in the speech of God.

Malachi is grouped in the second of the threefold division of books in the Jewish Bible, but it is the concluding book of the Old Testament in the Christian Bible – the last of the prophets, foreshortening for later readers the years before the birth of Christ.

Bible quotations are taken from the NRSV.

# 1 Corruption at the heart of worship

### Malachi 1

Well before the time of the book of Malachi, the sibling rivalry between Esau and Jacob had come to epitomise the disjunctures in the histories of two related nations. Jacob (or Israel) survives again and again despite self-inflicted tragedy, while Esau (Edom) is destroyed. God has made a covenant of blessing with Jacob, even though Jacob tricked Esau out of his birthright (Genesis 25:19–34): 'Yet I have loved Jacob but I have hated Esau' (vv. 2–3). 'Loved' and 'hated' might not be used here in the way we would use them, but they are terms which speak of preference and choice. This is the stumbling block that lies at the heart of 'special relationship'. In a way that would not have occurred to its first readers, we have to decide whether and how we can live with it.

The baseline of the book, though, is not a philosophical argument about fairness but an argument between God and God's people. It is a prophetic word conceived within a fractured relationship, where the people who are charged with keeping that relationship healthy are the ones who continue to do the most damage. The restoration of worship and ritual at the heart of a nation's life is seen to be hollow. Instead of bringing the perfect and unblemished sacrifices set out in the Law (Leviticus 22:19–25), the priests are bringing flawed offerings. They can't be bothered, so they are behaving as if God can't be bothered, as they bring to God what would be an insult to their provincial governor. The priests' example is so bad that God wishes that the temple doors were shut. It would be better not to worship at all. The sting of sarcasm cuts sharply into their complacency. They hear echoes of the Psalms proclaiming God's universal presence, but Malachi sounds a sharper tone: pure offerings are made in every (other) place, but God's own people profane their worship. We might compare verse 11 with Psalms 50:1; 113:3.

We may find it hard to relate to the religious sphere of this prophet's habitation. The strong social conscience of the eighth-century prophets seems to be less at the forefront in this post-exilic prophet. However, there is a strong connection between sincerity in ritual practice and its outworking in social behaviour, and we should be alert for this as we continue through the week's readings.

# 2 Fake worship

Vivid and shocking imagery is employed to illustrate the Lord's appalled reaction to the serial offenders who refuse to listen and to act on what they have been told God requires: 'I will rebuke your offspring, and spread dung on your faces, the dung of your offerings' (v. 3). The shock is compounded by the realisation that this most unclean of actions will be taken by God against those who set the greatest store by purity and cleanliness, the priests.

There is a proverb-like cadence in the despairing line, 'The lips of a priest should guard knowledge, and people should seek instruction from his mouth' (v. 7). The proverb tells a general truth, that there is a 'guarding' of knowledge and understanding which isn't a stockpiling of information but a preserving of what is important so that others may learn it. This is the unwritten contract of trust which undergirds the relationship between priest and people and makes it possible for them to work together for the good of their community. But here it is bankrupt. It wasn't always like this. There is a marker, from which they have fallen away. In this instance the 'marker' is the law and the priesthood together, a blend of instruction and practice, where 'do as I say' and 'do as I do' must belong together.

It sometimes helps to see a broad-brush picture before we pick away at the detail. The detail of the 'covenant with Levi' in these verses is a bit puzzling, since it is hard to find strong evidence of anything so specific. But all we need to see at this point is that he represents the true response of priesthood, which has been corrupted by those who inherited it.

We might also hear an echo of the sound of 'creation and fall' which inhabits the Old Testament in different ways, each of them inclining towards resolution in redemption. The creation of humankind and their grasping-falling, the creation of a people and their fall into disruption and exile, these are the broad brushstrokes; but the detail of the picture is given with many individual histories of God's call and people's flawed responses. We could read this lament over the priests in the same way. Those who were entrusted with the most important service have fallen away, but there is hope of redemption.

# 3 Faithless in relationship

Rhetorical questions often have more impact than flat statements. 'Have we not all one father? Has not one God created us? Why then are we faithless to one another, profaning the covenant of our ancestors?' (v. 10). The only answers which can be given by the people simply show that they have lost any sense of how things hold together well.

Sometimes, in answering their own questions, authors leave their later readers with a sense of incompleteness. A progression of questions draws us on, but we might stumble a little at the answer to 'What does the one God desire?' (v. 15). If we were expecting something more along the lines of Micah's ringing tones, 'to do justice, and to love kindness, and to walk humbly with your God' (Micah 6:8), we might find Malachi's answer, 'Godly offspring', a little flat, banal even. But we could do worse than recognise that offspring have to do with a continuing story, an ongoing family line.

Through these verses there is a weaving together of the threads of the divine-human relationship and the community relationships on which mortals rely for their well-being. There is an appeal to partners and families who have given up on one another and are finding their pleasure with others, and to a nation to return to a faithful relationship with God. In a whole society, we might conclude, both aspects are found in harmony and a fracture in either sphere will be felt in the other. The image of a marriage covenant is beloved by the Hebrew prophets, and while we should remember that we can't assume a simple correspondence between marriage then and now, there is a common theme of commitment and consequences.

Malachi's social and religious context sets him in an era when national leaders were urging Jewish men to divorce their Gentile wives, whose foreign gods were, they believed, undermining the covenant community. But he paints another part of the picture, where Jewish men had been divorcing the Jewish wives in order to marry Gentile women. The disruption of divorce and the disruption of violence are set together (v. 16, although the translation of these verses is notoriously tricky), and we see something of what we would now call his social conscience. The reality was that divorced women would generally be left unprotected and in poverty. For the prophet, their well-being must not be separated from temple-centred worship and instruction.

# 4 Advent

We generally hear the first two verses of this chapter in the Advent season, when we are already tuned in to Christmas festival preparations. Longing for the joy to begin, we miss the dark irony of the prophet and keep company with all those whose anticipation is misdirected. 'The messenger of the covenant in whom you delight' (v. 1) is an eagerly awaited figure whose coming will not be what the people expect.

Familiar tropes of a refiner's fire and fullers' soap are employed to show the extent of the purification and cleansing which is needed. And those of us who in our reading have felt estranged from the text because of its emphasis on ritual are a little closer to having our concerns addressed. Judgement will be swift on those who have oppressed the vulnerable and weak and, by so doing, have shown that they are not bothered about their Lord (v. 5).

If this book were a musical performance, we might hear a joyful melody of welcome breaking through, only to be interrupted by the darker notes of a more menacing theme. The sound of a love song is fleetingly present, only for the key to change immediately; but without it the drama would be flattened out into a series of threats. The remembered melody highlights the fact that there has been a relationship, that there still is a relationship, but each partner has such a different view of what it is that it seems no meeting place remains.

However, the people have not perished. They are still there, to be addressed by the prophet who can only point out that God does not change. There is no change in God's requirement to deal honestly and without trickery (not relying on sorcery, adultery or perjury), to be fair in employment and towards those who are disadvantaged (the widow, the orphan and the alien). But God's utter consistency is also the reason why the people have not perished. And the controversy continues.

# 5 A mutual turning

'Return to me, and I will return to you' (v. 7). It seems that God's turning to the people depends on their turning to him. But this is one part of a dual aspect, and if we look briefly to the conclusion of the book, we find that it ends abruptly with an acknowledgement that, in order to return, the people need help beyond their own resolution. The prophet Elijah will be sent to be an agent of change, to reconcile the generations and make possible the people's return to God.

We would like to hear the tone of voice in which the prophet imagines the people's question, 'How shall we return?' However, the answer is clear: don't hold back, don't rob God. God, who is the source of all, cannot be robbed, of course. Malachi knew that and so do we. But there is a reminder here for every society which has grown complacent in its expectations of wealth or comfort. Being miserly with what we consider to be ours is tantamount to robbery, since ultimately nothing is ours that does not come from God.

When ritual is hollow and worshippers grudgingly bring only part of what they owe the Lord in worship, there is deficit and decay in the natural world. Good ritual and good living belong together (compare Deuteronomy 11:13–15; 28:2–12). This insight is sometimes lost on us, troubled by the apparent connection between material prosperity and doing what God wants in our lives. We aren't the first to be so troubled; from Job to Jesus there is witness against making this a necessary connection. Those who 'worship rightly', in whom ritual and right living are not separated, are not always prosperous, their fields do not always crop, their blessings are not always apparent. And yet there is a connection between our worship and the world's well-being.

At a local art exhibition, I stood before a painting of grape pickers. There was a correspondence of colour between the workers and their harvest, a sense of harmony and movement, a promise of blessing. The shadows were troubling, though. They were the wrong colour and seemed to fall in the wrong place! So much so that they dominated the whole and I lost the sense of the foreground. For us, the foreground of Malachi's text may have to do with acknowledging the relationship between what we bring and what God gives.

# 6 The sun of righteousness and the return of Elijah

**Malachi 4**

According to rabbinic tradition, 'When the last prophets, Haggai, Zechariah and Malachi, died, the Holy Spirit departed from Israel.' This is recorded in the Toseftah, the collection of oral law and interpretation which stands alongside the Mishnah in Jewish tradition. Yet this silence of the prophets does not bring the end of history, but reveals another waiting for a final judgement and the appearance of a messianic figure, and in this waiting there is still hope for a turning.

In the 'sun of righteousness' (v. 2) we come across another image familiar to the Advent season, but which reveals a wider cultural interface in the world of the prophet. If we are only tuned in to a complete divide between 'God's people' and 'the nations', we might miss the fact that neither the Old nor the New Testament gives us reason to suppose that God's action in the world takes place in a bubble, and some of the Bible's abiding truths are fashioned from and expressed in borrowed insights. The Egyptian representation of the chief of the gods reaching down to earth to bless and judge would have been well known.

The book ends not so much with a resolution as with an open question of the shape of things to come. The grand sweep of threats and disaster have been ineffective in turning the people away from destruction, but the return of the prophet Elijah will effect a reconciliation. In Jewish households at the celebration of the Passover meal, a seat is left empty, ready for Elijah: a focus of hope and token of a coming age of peace. The church discovers this fulfilment in John the Baptiser's preparation for Christ, but we might also ask what sort of reconciliation is being promised through the anticipation of Elijah.

Who is this Elijah? Is he the fearless character whom Ahab called 'you troubler of Israel' (1 Kings 18:17)? Or the worn-out figure standing in the cave's entrance at the raging of the storm, still to hear the sound of silence and the whisper of God? Which aspect of Elijah's story might best point to the renewal of relationship between parents and children as a sign that there is still hope for a renewal of relationship between God and the people he has created? Was it the compassionate action of saving the widow and her son from starvation, or was it the dramatic tradition of his departure, borne away on God's fiery chariot through flame and wind?

# Guidelines

- 'The priests' example is so bad that God wishes that the temple doors were shut. It would be better not to worship at all.' This speaks to those who recognise abusive or corrupt practices in the church, or discover that churches and Christian organisations are still investing in industries which are destructive to the created world. The challenge of Malachi 1:10 cuts to the heart of what we think we are doing in worship. These notes were being prepared in a period of national lockdown, as palpable anxiety was being held in tension with the desire to meet and gather again as we used to. For some, it became an impulse to take time to consider what we do and why we do it when we come together in worship. Can we use a period such as this to ask how we can purify our worship from seeking only our own satisfaction?

- Think of some of the 'relationship breakers' which Malachi mentions: second-rate offerings and the worship offered by dirty hands; abusive priests and ministers; and the wealth of the church in the midst of poverty. We don't have to look far to make connections. But those who bring their calling into disrepute do not destroy the significance of the covenant. Can you recall a time when someone you know and care for said that they no longer had any patience with Christian belief because of many clear examples of corruption and abuse within the church? How do you respond to this?

**FURTHER READING**

Joyce G. Baldwin, *Haggai, Zechariah and Malachi: An introduction and commentary* (IVP, 1972).

Gordon D. Fee and Robert L. Hubbard Jr (eds), *The Eerdmans Companion to the Bible*, commentary by Connie Gundry Tappy (Eerdmans, 2011).

Ingrid E. Lilly, 'Malachi', in Carol A. Newsom, Sharon H. Ringe and Jacqueline E. Lapsley (eds), *Women's Bible Commentary*, third edition (Westminster John Knox Press, 2012).

Gordon McConville, *Exploring the Old Testament, Vol. 4: The prophets* (SPCK, 2002).

# Become a Friend of BRF
## and give regularly
## to support our ministry

## We help people of all ages to grow in faith

We encourage and support individual Christians and churches as they serve and resource the changing spiritual needs of communities today.

Through **Anna Chaplaincy**
we're enabling churches to provide
spiritual care to older people

Through **Living Faith**
we're nurturing faith and resourcing
life-long discipleship

Through **Messy Church**
we're helping churches to reach out
to families

Through **Parenting for Faith**
we're supporting parents as they raise
their children in the Christian faith

Our ministry is only possible because of the generous support of individuals, churches, trusts and gifts in wills.

As we look to the future and make plans, **regular donations make a huge difference** in ensuring we can both start and finish projects well.

By becoming a Friend of BRF and giving regularly to our ministry you are partnering with us in the gospel and helping change lives.

# How your gift makes a difference

**£2**
a month

Helps us to develop **Living Faith** resources to use in care homes and communities

**£10**
a month

Helps us to support churches running the **Parenting for Faith** course and stand alongside parents

**£5**
a month

Helps us to support **Messy Church** volunteers and resource and grow the wider network

**£20**
a month

Helps us to resource **Anna Chaplaincy** and improve spiritual care for older people

 # How to become a Friend of BRF

Set up a Direct Debit donation at **brf.org.uk/donate** or find out how to set up a Standing Order at **brf.org.uk/friends**

**Contact the fundraising team**

Email:   **giving@brf.org.uk**
Tel:     +44 (0)1235 462305
Post:    Fundraising team, BRF, 15 The Chambers, Vineyard, Abingdon OX14 3FE

## Good to know

If you have any questions, or if you want to change your regular donation or stop giving in the future, do get in touch.

## SHARING OUR VISION – MAKING A ONE-OFF GIFT

**I would like to make a donation to support BRF.**
**Please use my gift for:**

☐ Where it is most needed   ☐ Anna Chaplaincy   ☐ Living Faith
☐ Messy Church   ☐ Parenting for Faith

| Title | First name/initials | Surname |
|-------|---------------------|---------|
| Address | | |
| | | Postcode |
| Email | | |
| Telephone | | |
| Signature | | Date |

Our ministry is only possible because of the generous support of individuals, churches, trusts and gifts in wills.

*giftaid it*   You can add an extra 25p to every £1 you give.

**Please treat as Gift Aid donations all qualifying gifts of money made**

☐ today,   ☐ in the past four years,   ☐ and in the future.

I am a UK taxpayer and understand that if I pay less Income Tax and/or Capital Gains Tax in the current tax year than the amount of Gift Aid claimed on all my donations, it is my responsibility to pay any difference.

☐ My donation does not qualify for Gift Aid.

Please notify BRF if you want to cancel this Gift Aid declaration, change your name or home address, or no longer pay sufficient tax on your income and/or capital gains.

Please complete other side of form ➲

## SHARING OUR VISION – MAKING A ONE-OFF GIFT

**Please accept my gift of:**

☐ £2 ☐ £5 ☐ £10 ☐ £20 Other £ ☐

by (*delete as appropriate*):

☐ Cheque/Charity Voucher payable to 'BRF'

☐ MasterCard/Visa/Debit card/Charity card

Name on card

Card no. ☐☐☐☐ ☐☐☐☐ ☐☐☐☐ ☐☐☐☐ ☐☐☐☐

Expires end [M][M] [Y][Y] Security code* ☐☐☐

*Last 3 digits on the reverse of the card
ESSENTIAL IN ORDER TO PROCESS
YOUR PAYMENT

Signature | Date

☐ I would like to leave a gift to BRF in my will.
Please send me further information.

For help or advice regarding making a gift, please contact
our fundraising team +44 (0)1865 462305

**Your privacy**

We will use your personal data to process this transaction.
From time to time we may send you information about
the work of BRF that we think may be of interest to you.
Our privacy policy is available at **brf.org.uk/privacy**.
Please contact us if you wish to discuss your mailing
preferences.

Registered with

(FR)

FUNDRAISING
**REGULATOR**

 Please complete other side of form

**Please return this form to 'Freepost BRF'**
*No other address information or stamp is needed*

BRF

The Bible Reading Fellowship is a Registered Charity (233280)

GL0321

*Overleaf…* *Guidelines* forthcoming issue | Author profile |
Recommended reading | Order and subscription forms

# *Guidelines* forthcoming issue

HELEN PAYNTER

As usual, at about the time that we sign off one issue of *Guidelines*, I am reading through the submissions for the following issue. I am excited about what we will be offering you next time. We have a happy mix of deep dives into biblical books (Steve Walton on Galatians, Pauline Hoggarth on Esther and Alison Lo on Kings), season specific reflections (David Kerrigan on 'travelling people' and David Spriggs on suffering, both for Lent; and John Rackley and Jenny Hellyer on Easter), and thematic reflections. I'm pleased that we will be able to offer three sets of reflections in a new occasional series called 'Milestones'. New writer Imogen Ball will be reflecting on pregnancy and childbirth and Ernest Lucas on old age. We also have helpful notes from Rosie Button on self care, and some thought-provoking reflections from Andy Angel around where we find God in the Covid crisis. Once again, I believe we have a rich feast to offer, and I hope you will join us at the table!

# What the Bible means to me: Stephen Finamore

The Bible matters to me because it enables me to understand who I am. It tells me about all the most fundamental relationships that define me. It offers an account of my purpose and my destiny. There may be many other stories, books and ideologies that claim to do these things, but they all leave me unconvinced. In them I find myself described in terms that make me either too good or too bad, too important or too insignificant, too powerful or too powerless. Only the Bible tells a story that coheres with my experience of myself and of the world. It's the only resource I've found that puts into words realities I would otherwise struggle to express. The Bible reminds me of truths about humanity that I would rather hide from and yet also enables me to grasp things I too easily forget. And it does this by telling me about God.

Astonishingly, the Bible accomplishes all of this without being a textbook, an almanac or a compilation of aphorisms. It mostly does it through stories, through poetry and through guidelines and letters addressed to other people. There are other books I've read more than once but no others that I turn to every day and discover, no matter how many times I've seen the words before, fresh insights. The text strips back the layers of human desires, motivations and pretensions so that I stand utterly exposed in its light. Yet at the same time it whispers to me that the maker of the cosmos, who is self-giving love and who gives meaning and purpose to all things, cherishes me and gives my life meaning and a sense of purpose.

That a collection of texts from distant cultures, written in foreign languages and gathered from across many centuries, should speak in such ways in its own day and in every day since, is simply remarkable. In such circumstances, it is little wonder that I and many others have learned to trust in the Bible as the word of God. Its impact cannot be accounted for in purely human terms. However much it may be a set of human texts that emerged in particular times and places for reasons that range from the astonishing to the banal, the Bible is also something that speaks to us from beyond. It prises open our closed worlds and exposes us to the possibilities of transcendence.

So the Bible inevitably means a great deal to me. One of my tasks is to teach it, so in one sense it represents my livelihood – it both is and earns my daily bread. But much more than that, it is my means of understanding and orienting myself. I recall, many years ago, preparing to go overseas with Tearfund to be involved in rural development work in the Peruvian Andes. One of the trainers was talking about the *Oxfam Field Director's Handbook* and explaining – jokingly, to be fair – that this would be our Bible. He meant it would be an indispensable guide to the development work we were doing, how we were doing it and even why we were doing it. It's a great book, but I have to say that he was wrong. The Bible is my Bible, my indispensable guide to what, how and why.

# Recommended reading

Advent is a time to remember and reflect on the Christmas story and the baby at its heart. But the virgin birth, the manger, the mysterious eastern visitors and their portentous gifts – all these hint at a much grander narrative. Come and explore the whole Christmas story, and find your place within it.

The following is an edited extract from the introduction to *The Whole Christmas Story*, by Jo Swinney.

When we talk about the Christmas story, we are generally covering the ground between the angel Gabriel's visit to Mary and Joseph, Mary and Jesus' escape to Egypt. These events are recounted in the gospels of Matthew and Luke: 120 verses between them. The details are few and familiar. A young virgin suddenly pregnant, her fiancé shamed. A reassuring dream for Joseph and a soothing visit to an older relative for Mary. A journey to a far-off town for a census, the discovery that all guest rooms are full and the newborn Jesus laid in a manger. A visit from some shepherds and the Magi, whose arrival alerts King Herod to a pretender to his throne.

Understandably, at this time of year we think a great deal about this story. You might imagine a book created to help you engage with the season on a spiritual level would take you through the relevant sections of Matthew and Luke, perhaps coming at them at a new angle or showing them in a different light. There are many wonderful Advent devotionals that do this. I have used them and found them helpful.

But I want to do something different here. I want us to think about how Christmas sits in the whole Christian story, from Genesis to Revelation. I want to take us up a steep and winding path to a high vantage point, from where we can survey the horizon in all directions. Or, to use a more specifically 21st-century metaphor, let's play with Google Earth, starting in outer space and zooming in further and further until we are sitting, mesmerised and wor-shipful by a makeshift cradle and the God-baby inside it. Who is Jesus, and what is his cosmic significance? Who was he to the generations who came and went before his birth, and who is he to those of us living long after? Why did God take on human form, and what do we do with all those not completely fulfilled promises of healing and deliverance?

Please don't expect tidy answers to those huge questions in these pages. They aren't there. But the Bible does take us into the heart of God's purposes for his creation and if we come humbly and open to the task, he will open our eyes as we read and explore over this Advent season.

On a personal note, I have to confess that, over the years, hearing the Christmas story told in a secular context has sometimes made me cringe a bit inside. It all seemed so far-fetched when given an airing among purportedly rational, educated and sophisticated people: a quaint and primitive fairy story for those willing to suspend disbelief in the name of faith. I wondered if in my heart of hearts, I actually believed it. I suspected it would take a real test to show me my true mettle as a self-professed Jesus follower.

I started work on this book in September 2019. On 28 October, just under two months later, I spent the morning writing. I was on track to hand in a completed manuscript by my January deadline and my mum, who has worked with me on all my books, was in the wings to go through an early draft as soon as I had one to give her.

After lunch, I did a superficial house tidy and packed for a few days away. Around 3.30 pm, I set off with my husband, Shawn, and our daughters, Alexa and Charis, for a half-term break in a remote cottage we had rented. My husband Shawn's phone rang five minutes into our journey, as we were driving down a steep road outside Bath called Brassknocker Hill. It was my uncle Steve, and he asked Shawn to pull over and give him a call back.

Once they had spoken, Shawn got back in the car with red eyes and said we had to go back home. Something really bad had happened, and he'd tell us what it was when we had got into the house. Both girls started crying and asking questions. I told them whatever the news was, God was good, and he loved us, and we'd be okay.

The news was life-altering. My parents had been in a terrible car accident in South Africa, where they had been on a work trip with the charity they had founded, A Rocha. My mother had been killed along with two colleagues and friends, Chris and Susanna Naylor. The driver was alive, and my father was in critical condition. I'm so glad I can tell you he miraculously survived with no long-term physical injuries.

Subsequent weeks and months have been painful and dark. Grief hits me like a kind of reverse labour, with contractions coming further apart with time. The intensity of loss can take my breath away, but it recedes and somehow life goes on.

Even at the beginning, when there was barely a second's reprieve from howling hurt and shock, I had no questions for God. I realised my belief that he was real, he was good and he was loving went deep. I sensed the Holy Spirit brooding over the troubled waters of my distress. Silent, yes, but present, working redemption even as I thrashed around, fearing I'd drown.

My mum loved Christmas. She would start playing wall to wall carols on 1 December (we'd banned her from starting earlier), bake dozens of mince pies and spend hours lovingly wrapping the gifts she'd been stockpiling all year. Our Christmas tree was always the best tree of all the trees, and she'd often sit in the glow of its lights late in the evening in childlike delight.

We did our best to celebrate our first Christmas without her, telling ourselves she'd have wanted us to give the grandchildren a happy day. Without her, our clan numbers 17, and we were all together. I'm not sure we celebrated, but we managed to get through it. Christmas without her is never going to be the same.

One thing I know: the Christmas baby has given me a sure and certain hope that one day I will see her again and we will be together in the unveiled presence of the triune God. As Zechariah said after the birth of his own miraculous son, John, Jesus has given us 'salvation through the forgiveness of [our] sins, because of the tender mercy of our God, by which the rising sun will come to us from heaven to shine on those living in darkness and in the shadow of death' (Luke 1:77–79). This is the big picture. This is the context. This is how the whole thing makes sense.

*To order a copy of this book, please use the order form on page 151 or visit brfonline.org.uk.*

'Comfort, O comfort my people, says your God...' Through nine reflections, Steven Croft examines what these 'comfortable words' have to say to us. Each reflection begins from a passage of scripture taken from Isaiah 40—55: the song of an unnamed prophet who sings at the end of the exile to call God's people home. These are comfortable words the whole world needs to hear afresh in this season.

**Comfortable Words**
*A call to restoration: Reflections on Isaiah 40—55*
Steven Croft
978 1 80039 105 5   £7.99
brfonline.org.uk

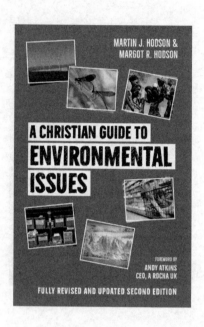

MARTIN J. HODSON &
MARGOT R. HODSON

# A CHRISTIAN GUIDE TO
# ENVIRONMENTAL
# ISSUES

FOREWORD BY
ANDY ATKINS
CEO, A ROCHA UK

**FULLY REVISED AND UPDATED SECOND EDITION**

In this extensively updated edition, Martin and Margot Hodson consider eight of the key current environmental problems, giving the biblical basis for looking after the environment and helping to integrate environmental thinking into the reader's understanding of Christian faith. This accessible guide includes ethical reflections, Bible studies focusing on a different biblical doctrine for each chapter, and eco-tips to enable practical response.

**A Christian Guide to Environmental Issues**
Martin J. Hodson and Margot R. Hodson
978 1 80039 005 8  £9.99
brfonline.org.uk

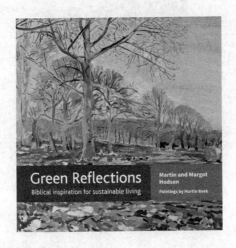

How should we look after the world we inhabit? Martin and Margot Hodson bring together scientific and theological wisdom to offer 62 reflections inspired by passages from the Bible in a thoughtful exploration that encourages both reflection and response. Themes include The Wisdom of Trees, Landscapes of Promise and Sharing Resources.

**Green Reflections**
*Biblical inspiration for sustainable living*
Martin and Margot Hodson
978 1 80039 068 3  £8.99
brfonline.org.uk

# Deep Calls to Deep

**Spiritual formation
in the hard places of life**

Tony Horsfall

The Psalms offer honest insights into the reality of life with God, reflecting every human emotion and situation. Through some of the Psalms written 'from the depths' we can understand more fully the way God works to shape our characters and form the life of Christ within us during difficult times in life. This will enable us not only to make sense of our own history with God, but also help us to get to know God here and now, and prepare us for what may lie ahead.

**Deep Calls to Deep**
*Spiritual formation in the hard places of life*
Tony Horsfall
978 1 80039 066 9  £8.99
brfonline.org.uk

# o order

Delivery times within the UK are
normally 15 working days. Prices are
correct at the time of going to press
but may change without prior notice.

| tle | Price | Qty | Total |
|---|---|---|---|
| he Whole Christmas Story | £8.99 | | |
| he BRF Book of 365 Bible Reflections | £14.99 | | |
| omfortable Words | £7.99 | | |
| Christian Guide to Environmental Issues | £9.99 | | |
| reen Reflections | £8.99 | | |
| eep Calls to Deep | £8.99 | | |

| POSTAGE AND PACKING CHARGES | | | |
|---|---|---|---|
| der value | UK | Europe | Rest of world |
| der £7.00 | £2.00 | | |
| 00–£29.99 | £3.00 | Available on request | Available on request |
| ).00 and over | FREE | | |

| | |
|---|---|
| Total value of books | |
| Donation* | |
| Postage and packing | |
| **Total for this order** | |

\* Please complete and return the
Gift Aid declaration on page 139.

## ase complete in BLOCK CAPITALS

itle _____ First name/initials _____ Surname _____

ddress _____

_____ Postcode _____

cc. No. _____ Telephone _____

mail _____

## Method of payment

☐ Cheque (made payable to BRF)  ☐ MasterCard / Visa

ard no. ☐☐☐☐ ☐☐☐☐ ☐☐☐☐ ☐☐☐☐

xpires end ☐☐ ☐☐  Security code* ☐☐☐  Last 3 digits on the reverse
of the card

ignature* _____ Date _____ /_____ /_____
ESSENTIAL IN ORDER TO PROCESS YOUR ORDER

## ease return this form to:
'F, 15 The Chambers, Vineyard, Abingdon OX14 3FE | **enquiries@brf.org.uk**
read our terms and find out about cancelling your order, please visit **brfonline.org.uk/terms**.

The Bible Reading Fellowship (BRF) is a Registered Charity (233280)

# BRF needs you!

If you're one of our regular *Guidelines* readers, you will know all about the rich rewards of regular Bible study and the value of serious daily notes to guide, inform and challenge you.

Here are some recent comments from *Guidelines* readers:

'... *very thoughtful and spiritually helpful. [These notes] are speaking to the church as it is today, and therefore to Christians like us who live in today's world.*'

'*You have assembled an amazingly diverse group of people and their contributions are most certainly thoughtful.*'

If you have similarly positive things to say about *Guidelines*, would you be willing to help spread the word about these valuable resources? One suggestion is to form a *Guidelines* reading group, not to take the place of private Bible study and prayer, but to give group members a chance to discover new dimensions and different interpretations as well as make new friends. It could be a breakfast or lunchtime meeting: short and to the point, or a more relaxed encounter, over a meal or a drink.

It doesn't need to be complicated: all *Guidelines* study notes have questions for reflection and suggestions for additional reading that lend themselves to group exploration.

We can supply further information if you need it and would love to hear about it if you do start a *Guidelines* reading group.

For more information:

- Email **enquiries@brf.org.uk**
- Telephone BRF on +44 (0)1865 319700 Mon–Fri 9.30–17.00
- Write to us at BRF, 15 The Chambers, Vineyard, Abingdon OX14 3FE

# Enabling all ages to grow in faith

At BRF, we long for people of all ages to grow in faith and understanding of the Bible. That's what all our work as a charity is about.

- Our **Living Faith** range of resources helps Christians go deeper in their understanding of scripture, in prayer and in their walk with God. Our conferences and events bring people together to share this journey. Our Holy Habits resources help whole congregations grow together as disciples of Jesus, living out and sharing their faith.

- We also want to make it easier for local churches to engage effectively in ministry and mission – by helping them bring new families into a growing relationship with God through **Messy Church** or by supporting churches as they nurture the spiritual life of older people through **Anna Chaplaincy**.

- Our **Parenting for Faith** team coaches parents and others to raise God-connected children and teens, and enables churches to fully support them.

## Do you share our vision?

Though a significant proportion of BRF's funding is generated through our charitable activities, we are dependent on the generous support of individuals, churches and charitable trusts.

If you share our vision, would you help us to enable even more people of all ages to grow in faith? Your prayers and financial support are vital for the work that we do. You could:

- Support BRF's ministry with a regular donation;
- Support us with a one-off gift;
- Consider leaving a gift to BRF in your will (see page 154);
- Encourage your church to support BRF as part of your church's giving to home mission – perhaps focusing on a specific ministry or programme;
- Most important of all, support BRF with your prayers.

Donate at **brf.org.uk/donate** or use the form on pages 139–40.

# Speaking and sharing good news with vulnerable, yet valued, members of society

There was also a prophet, Anna, the daughter of Penuel, of the tribe of Asher. She was very old... She never left the temple but worshipped night and day, fasting and praying. Coming up to them at that very moment, she gave thanks to God and spoke about the child to all who were looking forward to the redemption of Jerusalem.

LUKE 2:36–38 (NIV, abridged)

**Anna Chaplaincy**
for older people

When Jesus was brought to the temple and after Simon uttered his famous prayer, Anna steps into the limelight and prophesies of the redemption of Jerusalem. It is from Anna that BRF's ministry – Anna Chaplaincy for Older People – draws its name. Anna spoke of redemption, hope and God's good plan.

It is this same hope that more than 150 Anna Chaplains seek to share with older people across the country. While the pandemic hindered face-to-face ministry, God found a way. One Anna Chaplain, Elizabeth, conducted mini services with one person after another by phone. She read a Bible passage, sang hymns and offered prayers and thanksgivings. Many others found ways to continue ministering at this trying time.

Anna Chaplains help older people in care remain connected to other people and to those aspects of life which bring meaning and purpose to them.

Sustaining and growing this ministry is only possible because of generous donations from donors, churches, charitable trusts and gifts in wills. You can find out more at **brf.org.uk/annachaplaincy**. Please consider whether you or your church could support this ministry financially. You can get in touch with the fundraising team via **giving@brf.org.uk**, on 01235 462305 or by post. Your prayers, as ever, are hugely appreciated.

> Pray. Give. Get involved.
> **brf.org.uk**

## GUIDELINES SUBSCRIPTION RATES

Please note our new subscription rates, current until 30 April 2022:

**Individual subscriptions**
covering 3 issues for under 5 copies, payable in advance
(including postage & packing):

|  | UK | Europe | Rest of world |
| --- | --- | --- | --- |
| *Guidelines* 1-year subscription | £18.00 | £25.95 | £29.85 |
| *Guidelines* 3-year subscription (9 issues) | £52.65 | N/A | N/A |

**Group subscriptions**
covering 3 issues for 5 copies or more, sent to one UK address (post free):

| *Guidelines* 1-year subscription | £14.25 per set of 3 issues p.a. |
| --- | --- |

Please note that the annual billing period for group subscriptions runs from 1 May to 30 April.

**Overseas group subscription rates**
Available on request. Please email **enquiries@brf.org.uk**.

Copies may also be obtained from Christian bookshops:

| *Guidelines* | £4.75 per copy |
| --- | --- |

All our Bible reading notes can be ordered online
by visiting **brfonline.org.uk/subscriptions**

**GUIDELINES**

*Guidelines* is also available as
an app for Android, iPhone and iPad
**brfonline.org.uk/apps**

## GUIDELINES INDIVIDUAL SUBSCRIPTION FORM

All our Bible reading notes can be ordered online by visiting
**brfonline.org.uk/subscriptions**

☐ I would like to take out a subscription:

Title ............ First name/initials ............... Surname ...............................
Address ..............................................................................................
............................................................... Postcode ...........................
Telephone ......................... Email ...............................................

Please send *Guidelines* beginning with the January 2022 / May 2022 /
September 2022 issue (*delete as appropriate*):

| (*please tick box*) | UK | Europe | Rest of world |
|---|---|---|---|
| *Guidelines* 1-year subscription | ☐ £18.00 | ☐ £25.95 | ☐ £29.85 |
| *Guidelines* 3-year subscription | ☐ £52.65 | N/A | N/A |

Optional donation to support the work of BRF £ ...................

Total enclosed £ ................... (cheques should be made payable to 'BRF')

Please complete and return the Gift Aid declaration on page 139 to make your
donation even more valuable to us.

Please charge my MasterCard / Visa ☐ Debit card ☐ with £ ...................

Card no. ☐☐☐☐ ☐☐☐☐ ☐☐☐☐ ☐☐☐☐

Expires end ☐☐ ☐☐    Security code* ☐☐☐    Last 3 digits on the reverse
of the card

Signature* ....................................................... Date ....../....../......
*ESSENTIAL IN ORDER TO PROCESS YOUR PAYMENT

To set up a Direct Debit, please also complete the Direct Debit instruction
on page 159 and return it to BRF with this form.

**Please return this form to:**
BRF, 15 The Chambers, Vineyard, Abingdon OX14 3FE

To read our terms and find out about cancelling your order, please visit **brfonline.org.uk/terms**.

The Bible Reading Fellowship (BRF) is a Registered Charity (233280)

GL0321

## GUIDELINES GIFT SUBSCRIPTION FORM

☐ I would like to give a gift subscription (please provide both names and addresses):

Title ............ First name/initials .............. Surname ............................

Address ..................................................................................

.................................................................. Postcode ..................

Telephone ........................... Email ................................................

Gift subscription name ...................................................................

Gift subscription address ................................................................

.................................................................. Postcode ..................

Gift message (20 words max. or include your own gift card):

..........................................................................................

..........................................................................................

Please send *Guidelines* beginning with the January 2022 / May 2022 / September 2022 issue *(delete as appropriate)*:

| *(please tick box)* | UK | Europe | Rest of world |
|---|---|---|---|
| *Guidelines* 1-year subscription | ☐ £18.00 | ☐ £25.95 | ☐ £29.85 |
| *Guidelines* 3-year subscription | ☐ £52.65 | N/A | N/A |

Optional donation to support the work of BRF £ ...........................

Total enclosed £ ........................... (cheques should be made payable to 'BRF')

Please complete and return the Gift Aid declaration on page 139 to make your donation even more valuable to us.

Please charge my MasterCard / Visa ☐ Debit card ☐ with £ ................

Card no. ☐☐☐☐ ☐☐☐☐ ☐☐☐☐ ☐☐☐☐

Expires end ☐☐ ☐☐   Security code* ☐☐☐   Last 3 digits on the reverse of the card

Signature* ............................................... Date ....... /....... /.......

*ESSENTIAL IN ORDER TO PROCESS YOUR PAYMENT

To set up a Direct Debit, please also complete the Direct Debit instruction on page 159 and return it to BRF with this form.

**Please return this form to:**
BRF, 15 The Chambers, Vineyard, Abingdon OX14 3FE

**BRF**

To read our terms and find out about cancelling your order, please **visit brfonline.org.uk/terms**.
The Bible Reading Fellowship (BRF) is a Registered Charity (233280)

You can pay for your annual subscription to our Bible reading notes using Direct Debit. You need only give your bank details once, and the payment is made automatically every year until you cancel it. If you would like to pay by Direct Debit, please use the form opposite, entering your BRF account number under 'Reference number'.

You are fully covered by the Direct Debit Guarantee:

---

### The Direct Debit Guarantee

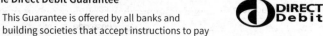

- This Guarantee is offered by all banks and building societies that accept instructions to pay Direct Debits.
- If there are any changes to the amount, date or frequency of your Direct Debit, The Bible Reading Fellowship will notify you 10 working days in advance of your account being debited or as otherwise agreed. If you request The Bible Reading Fellowship to collect a payment, confirmation of the amount and date will be given to you at the time of the request.
- If an error is made in the payment of your Direct Debit, by The Bible Reading Fellowship or your bank or building society, you are entitled to a full and immediate refund of the amount paid from your bank or building society.
- If you receive a refund you are not entitled to, you must pay it back when The Bible Reading Fellowship asks you to.
- You can cancel a Direct Debit at any time by simply contacting your bank or building society. Written confirmation may be required. Please also notify us.

---

The Bible Reading Fellowship

# Instruction to your bank or building society to pay by Direct Debit

Please fill in the whole form using a ballpoint pen and return it to:
BRF, 15 The Chambers, Vineyard, Abingdon OX14 3FE

Service User Number: | 5 | 5 | 8 | 2 | 2 | 9 |

Name and full postal address of your bank or building society

| To: The Manager | Bank/Building Society |
| Address | |
| | |
| | Postcode |

Name(s) of account holder(s)

Branch sort code

Bank/Building Society account number

Reference number

**Instruction to your Bank/Building Society**
Please pay The Bible Reading Fellowship Direct Debits from the account detailed in this instruction, subject to the safeguards assured by the Direct Debit Guarantee. I understand that this instruction may remain with The Bible Reading Fellowship and, if so, details will be passed electronically to my bank/building society.

Signature(s)

Banks and Building Societies may not accept Direct Debit instructions for some types of account.

*Enabling all ages to grow in faith*

Anna Chaplaincy

Living Faith

Messy Church

Parenting for Faith

**The Bible Reading Fellowship (BRF)** is a Christian charity that resources individuals and churches. Our vision is to enable people of all ages to grow in faith and understanding of the Bible and to see more people equipped to exercise their gifts in leadership and ministry.

**To find out more about our work, visit**

brf.org.uk